U.S. Constitution: Preparing for the Test

BY
GEORGE LEE

ISBN 1-58037-138-8

Printing No. CD-1360

Mark Twain Media, Inc., Publishers
Distributed by Carson-Dellosa Publishing Company, Inc.

Table of Contents

Introduction

A wise parent takes his or her small child to a park. The child wants to go down the tall slide, but the parent tells the child it isn't safe, and lets him or her go down the shorter slide instead. The child wants to swing high up into the clouds, but the parent pushes the swing up to a height where the youngster can enjoy the ride, but not so high that he or she is in danger. The child wants to do many things at the park, but the wise parent knows there are things that are too dangerous or risky to do. The child may not appreciate the parent at that moment, but in time, he or she will realize that restraint is better than a trip to the doctor or the hospital.

There are many things in life people want to do, but they need the guidance of someone wiser to prevent them from doing those things. The government of the United States is like that child in the park. It may want to do something foolish or dangerous, but the men who wrote the Constitution, the wise parents in our example, tell the government it cannot do those things. For over 200 years, the nation has been guided by the principles they set down. They made mistakes, some of which have been corrected by amendments to the Constitution and others by a broader interpretation by the courts, but their general principles still stand. It was a most remarkable group of men, and they accomplished one of mankind's greatest achievements.

There have been times when individuals have wanted to violate the provisions of the Constitution, but the nation has refused to allow them to ignore the instructions given so long ago during a hot summer in 1787. The style of writing of the Constitution may trouble you at times, but after you have read it and the explanations provided in this book, you will be able to understand what the creators of the Constitution meant.

As a young person now and an adult later, you will have the opportunity to participate in the nation's decision-making process as a citizen, a voter, possibly as a government employee, or perhaps even as an officeholder. How well you understand the principles by which the United States is governed will determine how well you participate as a citizen of this great nation.

The Constitution, the Bill of Rights, and the Declaration of Independence are displayed in the National Archives Building in Washington, D.C.

Information on the Format Followed in This Book

The first four chapters of this book contain background information on the history of the United States at the time of the Constitutional Convention. This is provided to help you understand the reasons why the Constitution was needed and the compromises that were made in order to get the Constitution formulated and ratified.

As you begin to study the Constitution, you should have a copy of the Constitution to read along with these pages. The material in this book in normal type will be a paraphrase of the Constitution. *The italicized part is an explanation of how the provision is used in the government of the United States today, if it is different from what a person reading the text might assume it means.* Students need to realize that in actual process, some parts of the Constitution have been interpreted in different ways by the Supreme Court (for example: freedom of speech, press, and religion), and those areas cannot be covered in a book like this.

Those parts of the original Constitution that have no modern usage or have been changed by amendments are simply marked "Deleted." In the copy of the Constitution provided in this book, the italicized type indicates parts of the Constitution no longer in effect.

At the end of each unit, there is a short pre-test for you to use in checking whether you understand the information or not. Because they are longer and are of great importance in understanding the Constitution, Articles I and II will be split into two parts each. The amendments will also be divided into five groups.

A test has been provided that covers the Constitution and the amendments. Depending on your school or state requirements, this test may be used as the actual Constitution test for your class, or it may be used as a practice test to prepare for the required test.

Your teacher may want your class to discuss certain questions. Here are some possiblities:

1. Why is this provision in the Constitution? Who do you think might favor it? Who might oppose it? Why? If the American public had a chance to vote on it today, would it be included in the Constitution, changed, or dropped?
2. Notice the dates amendments were made. What was going on in the United States at that time that caused the Congress and states to ratify the amendments?
3. Ask the students to think about topics that might be included in an amendment today, and help them put it in a form that looks like other amendments to the Constitution.
4. Ask the students to watch in the newspaper and TV news programs for Supreme Court decisions interpreting the Constitution. Have them look at the Constitution to see what the basis for that decision is.
5. Challenge the class to memorize the second paragraph of the Declaration of Independence and the Preamble to the Constitution.
6. After finishing the book, create some situations for the class to discuss. For example, the President decides to call off the upcoming election because of a war, or Congress decides that newspapers criticize them too much, so it creates a watchdog group with the power to close any newspaper that causes public disapproval of Congress.

The Articles of Confederation

During the colonial period, people in the English colonies along the Eastern seaboard of North America did not call themselves "Americans," but thought of themselves as Pennsylvanians, New Yorkers, and so on. They had little contact with anyone outside their own counties; roads were poor or non-existent, and sea travel was slow. Newspapers were rare and carried very little besides local news anyway. A trip of 15 to 20 miles was a hard day's ride, so people in the eastern part of a colony sometimes knew little about what was happening in the western part of the colony.

The colony was ruled by a governor (usually appointed by the king), the Council (an upper house hand-chosen by the governor), and a lower house chosen by the people. The lower houses went by different names in different colonies, but for the most part, the members were wealthy, better-educated, and concerned about keeping taxes down and making sure the governor did not become too powerful. In time, these representatives became very suspicious of the king and Parliament and questioned their colonial policies.

After the French and Indian War ended in 1763, the British government needed money to pay off its national debt. It decided to (1) increase tax revenue and (2) bring the American colonies under stricter control. These ideas clashed with the colonists who began protesting "too much government" and "too many taxes." Many Americans felt they had had enough of British rule, and in 1775 fighting began in Massachusetts.

The colonies realized they must start working together, so they created the First Continental Congress in 1775 and, a year later, the Second Continental Congress. George Washington was chosen by the Second Congress to lead the Continental army, diplomats were sent to foreign countries, and the Declaration of Independence was approved. Everything happened so quickly that the colonies did not even have time to create a document that gave them the authority to do what they had already done.

The states had been ruled by colonial charters. Those were quickly set aside, and states started throwing out the old governors and Councils. The states wrote new constitutions that usually created two-house legislatures with members of both houses elected.[1] They chose new governors, but took away most of the governors' powers. Most governors were elected to one-year terms. Real power was in the hands of the legislature.

In 1777, the Articles of Confederation were written by John Dickinson. This document created a "league of friendship." The Articles united the states, but without any threat to their power. The Confederation would be run by a one-house Congress. It was to have the power to send diplomats, borrow money, and make treaties. Even then, some Americans feared this was creating a government in a distant place that might threaten their rights. Small states refused to approve it because some of the larger states had large land claims in the West. Until the large states gave up those lands, the small states would not approve. In 1781, Maryland agreed to approve the Articles after Virginia gave up its title to a large region in the West.

While debate over the Articles went on, General Washington had a war to fight and win. In 1781, the British were defeated at Yorktown. Except at some frontier forts, there were no British troops on American soil. In 1783, the British gave America its independence.

The states were officially united in a Confederation. Congress had a president, but he was only the presiding officer of Congress, not the national leader. The main weakness was that the Confederation Congress had no power to tax. It could request money from the states, and it did, but it had no power to demand money from the citizens or the states. Robert Livingston described the Confederation as a riddle, looking like a government to one man, and a creature of the states to another.

In a world of kings, emperors, and governors, the United States was alone in having no national leader. Also, the Confederation had no courts, so it had no way to enforce its policies. In order to make decisions, representatives from nine states had to approve; to change the Articles required approval by all thirteen states. The Confederation had so little power that some states forgot to send delegates; sometimes when delegates were appointed, they never attended a session. There were times when only three to five states were represented, and there was nothing for them to do but adjourn.

With a Confederation Congress lacking the power to solve problems, a large number of issues could not be solved. (1) Soldiers had not been paid, and Congress had no money to pay them. (2) States rarely sent any money to help pay the bills. Congress tried to solve that problem by putting out more money. An expression developed: "Not worth a continental" to describe the almost worthless paper money Congress issued. (3) The United States had borrowed large sums from France to fight the war. The French government desperately needed the money and kept asking for it to be repaid. (4) Spain was interested in taking lands west of the Appalachian mountains. (5) English troops remained in forts along the frontier. (6) Pirates were raiding American ships in the Mediterranean. (7) States were taxing goods being imported from foreign countries and other states. (8) Riots broke out threatening to destroy state governments. The worst rioting was in Massachusetts where Shays' Rebellion closed down courts. The militia put the rebellion down, and Shays escaped. In Rhode Island, debtor farmers took over the legislature and started putting out worthless paper money. New Hampshire's legislature had to be rescued after angry farmers surrounded the capitol building. In the views of many, unless something was done soon, the freedom gained by the Revolution would be lost.

[1] Pennsylvania was an exception. It chose an Executive Council to be the "governor," and a one-house legislature.

Name: ______________________ Date: ______________

Questions

Americans have always complained about government. Below are some complaints people might have had about the Confederation. Decide whether the complaint given would fit the Confederation, circle "YES" or "NO," and then tell why.

1. We don't know much about what's going on in the Confederation Congress. YES/NO Why?

   ____

   ____

   ____

2. The president of Congress is like the old colonial governors we threw out. YES/NO Why?

   ____

   ____

   ____

3. Congress has no power to make a treaty ending the war. YES/NO Why?

   ____

   ____

   ____

4. Congress has passed taxes so high no one can pay them. YES/NO Why?

   ____

   ____

   ____

5. Congress is always meeting and passing new bills. YES/NO Why?

   ____

   ____

   ____

Name: ______________________________ Date: ____________________

Questions (continued)

6. States are always being forced to send money to Congress. Don't they know that states can't send money without raising taxes, and we can't afford the taxes we have? YES/NO Why?

____

____

____

7. Those judges appointed by Congress are too powerful. YES/NO Why?

____

____

____

8. The British are still in forts on American soil. Shouldn't they leave? YES/NO Why?

____

____

____

9. Shays' Rebellion is an example of rich people threatening to overthrow state government. YES/NO Why?

____

____

____

10. If they chose me for Congress, I wouldn't go. They don't do anything at those meetings anyway. YES/NO Why?

____

____

____

Calling the Constitutional Convention

Imagine the thrill Jones felt when he opened an official-looking envelope informing him that he had been chosen to represent his state in the Confederation Congress. He showed it to his wife, and she said, "Who's going to run the farm while you are away?" He showed it to his children, and when he told them it meant he would be away for months at a time, they started crying. He showed it to the storekeeper, who laughed and said, "I have more money in my cash box than they have in their treasury." He talked to his state senator who told him ten other men had turned down the honor before it was offered to Jones. Then he reminded Jones that his salary was to come from the state, and before he did anything in Congress, he had better check with the state first. Otherwise, they might fire him or refuse to pay his expenses.

Jones took the job anyway and made the long trip to wherever Congress was meeting at the time. If he went by a sailing ship, there was no certainty when he would arrive. If he rode his horse, it meant several nights of lodging with farmers along the way or sleeping in flea-infested inns. At last he arrived and found there were not enough delegates present to do any business. Sometimes, only three to five delegations were there, and the Articles required that nine states be represented. After listening to the clerk read letters of complaint from former soldiers who needed to be paid or letters from ministers (ambassadors) in foreign countries telling them the ruler needed a payment on their debt, there was nothing more to do, so they adjourned. Tomorrow, perhaps enough delegates might arrive from other states so they could do some business. After a few weeks of this, Jones knew why the other ten men had turned down the honor of serving in this job. It did not take long for him to resign.

Jones was facing only a small portion of American problems however. States were having their troubles too. New Jersey was furious with a New York tax on eggs imported from other states. Virginia and Maryland argued over which was to control trade on the Potomac River. There were arguments over borders between Maryland and Pennsylvania. Each state acted only in its own interest and did not care about what was good for the nation. Westerners were furious about the Jay-Gardoqui (gar-do-key) treaty. It would allow American ships to trade with Spain, *if* the United States gave up use of the Mississippi River for 25 or 30 years. New England ship owners wanted the trade, but the westerner would have no way to get his goods to market. The Southern states sided with the West, and the treaty got only a 7 to 5 vote of approval, short of the number needed.

The rich and poor distrusted each other. The nation was divided between agricultural versus trading states. North and South argued over slavery. Big states like New York and Virginia thought they should have a bigger role in making decisions than small states like Delaware and Rhode Island. The unity that had won the Revolution was gone. Leaders like Washington, Madison, and Hamilton feared that, unless something happened soon, the nation would split apart.

To make the changes needed required taking advantage of opportunities to meet and discuss issues in a calm way. The first break occurred in 1785 when Maryland agreed to talk about trade on the Potomac River with Virginia. Washington invited the delegates to meet at his home, and the meeting became known as the MOUNT VERNON CONFERENCE. It went well, and as it was closing, James Madison suggested that it would be helpful if the trade problems between all the states could be discussed. A meeting was scheduled to do that, and it was to be held at Annapolis, Maryland.

Only five states sent delegates to the ANNAPOLIS CONVENTION in 1786. They were unable to do much, but Alexander Hamilton of New York and James Madison proposed that a meeting be held in 1787 at Philadelphia to consider ways to make the American government work better.

An event occurred at this point that had a great effect on what happened next. The state legislature of Massachusetts had raised taxes on land so high farmers could not survive. In 1786, Daniel Shays, a war veteran, led the farmers in attacks on court rooms where farmers were about to lose their land. When they marched to Springfield to take guns from the armory, they were stopped by a volley from militia. Washington and others recognized that incidents like this could occur throughout the country. Leaders began to see an urgency in sending delegates to Philadelphia. Congress gave its approval for the meeting on February 21, 1787, but only for "the purpose of revising the Articles of Confederation." By that time, five states had already chosen their delegates.

Most of those chosen took the assignment seriously. Washington did not want to make the trip, but felt he must; his decision to attend added importance to the gathering. Alexander Hamilton was known to favor a strong national government, so those in New York who favored strong state government sent two other delegates to keep Hamilton under control. James Wilson of Pennsylvania was one of America's best lawyers, and Roger Sherman of Connecticut was one of the best at putting a compromise together. Some delegates spent most of their time angry over something: Elbridge Gerry (Massachusetts) and Luther Martin (Maryland) in particular. To cool things down when tempers ran high was the genial Ben Franklin; his cheery disposition made people feel more at ease.

Sessions were supposed to begin May 14, but not enough of those chosen had arrived, so meetings did not begin until May 25. George Washington, to no one's surprise, was chosen president of the Convention.

No one knew what was going to happen as the doors closed, but the well-informed knew that life in America was about to change. They were right; a new form of government was about to be created.

Name: ______________________________ Date: ________________

Questions

Those who served in the Confederation Congress often stayed only a short time. Give three reasons Jones might have had for resigning.

1. ____

2. ____

3. ____

4. Why was New Jersey angry with New York?

____

____

5. Why were Westerners angry with John Jay?

____

____

6. Why did New Yorkers think they should have more influence than the states of Rhode Island or Delaware?

____

____

7. What was the purpose of the Mount Vernon Conference?

____

____

8. Why didn't the Annapolis Convention accomplish more?

____

____

9. What kind of government did Hamilton want?

____

____

10. Why would the presence of men like Roger Sherman be so important?

____

____

Drafting and Ratifying the Constitution

The Constitutional Convention gathering in Philadelphia in 1787 included many of the most brilliant, most experienced leaders in the country. George Washington, the hero of the Revolution, was chosen to preside. James Madison was later known as the "Father of the Constitution" because of his work at the Convention and getting the Constitution ratified. Roger Sherman rescued the Convention when tempers ran high over whether Congress was to be made up of equal delegations or on the basis of population. Others played less important roles but spoke up at the right time. For example, James Wilson suggested that the president be one person, not a committee. Gouverneur Morris was the most important member of the Committee of Style that put the Constitution in its final form.

Altogether, 73 delegates were chosen to attend the Convention, but only 55 ever came. Of those attending, eight were signers of the Declaration of Independence, about half had graduated from college, seven had been governors, 33 were lawyers, and many were quite young. The youngest was Jonathan Dayton of New Jersey who was 26; Alexander Hamilton was 32, James Madison was 36, and Ben Franklin was by far the oldest at 81.

Those coming often had strong opinions and prejudices, and many saw protecting their state's interests as their main duty. Tempers often flared during the sessions, and compromises had to be made. By the time the Convention ended, no delegate was completely happy with every clause in the Constitution, but most were convinced it was the best they could do.

There were some things, however, that they all agreed on. They all agreed that it was best to write out the Constitution rather than depend on an unwritten constitution like England did. They all agreed on a three-branch government (legislative, executive, and judicial) and in the separation of powers so each branch could operate independently of the others. They all wanted to produce a republican government, one where power rests with the people who directly or indirectly choose their leaders. They agreed that the national government must have the power to tax, to raise an army and navy, and conduct foreign policy. They agreed, with a few exceptions, that states must be an important part of the governing process in America. They understood the importance of what they were doing. Several issues were especially important to them and have been to the nation ever since.

Representation. The large states wanted representation in Congress to be based on population; the small states wanted every state to be equally represented in Congress. This issue came up early in the debates and almost tore the Convention apart. Finally, Roger Sherman came up with an idea that came to be known as the Great Compromise. The House of Representatives would be based on population, and the Senate would have an equal number of senators from each state.

The question then turned to whether slaves should count in representation. They finally compromised by agreeing to count a slave as three-fifths of a person. Each state was to decide who could and could not vote, except the Constitution stated that if a person could vote for a member to the lower house of the state legislature, he was to be allowed to vote for delegates to the House of Representatives.

Senators were to serve six-year terms; representatives were to serve two-year terms. Senators were chosen by state legislatures until the 17th Amendment was ratified in 1913.

The President. Only a few believed in splitting presidential authority between several people acting as an executive committee. Most wanted to have one person with that responsibility. Among issues that had to be settled were: (1) How long should he serve? (2) How should he be chosen? (3) How much power should he have? Governors had the closest office to the president, and they all served one- or two-year terms. The delegates decided the president was to have a four-year term and be eligible for re-election. The method of choosing the president was a big problem. Having voters choose him would become a popularity contest (remember that most people at that time had little to base their decisions on; many could not read, and others knew only a few names of leaders outside their states). Some suggested that he be chosen by Congress, but that would make him their puppet, violating the separation of powers principle.

After many hours of discussion, the issue was left to a committee, which came up with the idea of the ELECTORAL COLLEGE. Each state was to have a number of electors equal to the number of delegates to Congress. They would choose the president and vice president. How these electors were chosen was to be decided by the states.

Other important issues included taxation, slavery, the location of the national capital, the powers to be given to the courts, and whether to have a vice president and what he was supposed to do. One issue after another came up and was debated. When it appeared that about everything had been covered, a Committee of Style was created to put it all into a document. On September 17, 1787, the document was ready for signing. Of the 55 who had attended, 39 signed the finished product. Their work was not yet done, however. They would have to go back to their states and get the state to ratify (approve) it.

Ratification. Not everyone liked what they saw, and people divided between "Federalists" (those favoring it) and "Anti-Federalists" (those opposing it). Some important leaders lined up on both sides. The key states in the struggle, Virginia and New York, were the two largest. Virginia approved after James Madison assured the convention a bill of rights would be brought before Congress. In New York, the *Federalist Papers,* written by Madison, John Jay, and Alexander Hamilton helped swing the vote in favor of ratifying the Constitution.

Name: ______________________________ Date: ____________________

Questions

1. How many men took part in the Constitutional Convention?

____

2. Who became known as the "Father of the Constitution"?

____

3. What are the three branches of government?

____

____

4. What is a "republican form of government"?

____

____

5. How did the small states want Congress to be chosen?

____

____

6. How did the large states want Congress to be chosen?

____

____

7. What compromise did Sherman propose?

____

____

8. How many years does a senator serve? How many years does a member of the House of Representatives serve?

____

9. How many electors does a state have?

____

10. Who were the Anti-Federalists?

____

____

Understanding the Constitution

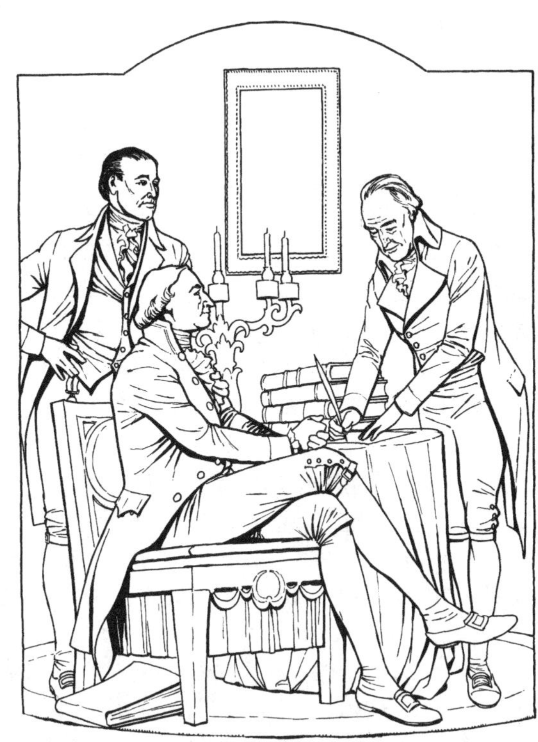

Many Americans, students and adults, think the Constitution is too hard to understand, and they give up on studying it before they even try. In fact, the Constitution can be easily understood if we remember a few basic facts. It was written in the 1780s by intelligent people who used the wording of their time, but the words have not changed that much in meaning. They were also practical people who produced a very logical means of governing a nation. They were experienced people who studied history and wanted to avoid mistakes that had endangered the freedom of the people in the past. They were not as concerned about giving powers as they were with preventing power from being abused.

Sol Bloom wrote: "Every American, as he studies the marvelous framework of the Constitution, can say with truth and pride: 'This was made for me. It is my fortress. When danger threatens my life or liberty I can take safe refuge in the Constitution. Into that fortress neither President nor Congress nor armies nor mobs can enter and take away my life or liberty.'" Unless we understand it, however, and defend its principles, our "fortress" crumbles, and our liberties can be lost. That is why you are taking the time to study the Constitution today.

Understanding a few basic principles will help your study of this amazing Constitution of the United States.

1. <u>Don't let anyone have too much power.</u> In the *Federalist Papers,* James Madison wrote: "If men were angels, no government would be necessary. If angels were to govern men, neither external nor internal control of government would be necessary. ... The great difficulty lies in this: you must first enable a government to control the governed; and in the next place, oblige it to control itself."

To make those in government control themselves, a clever system of <u>checks and balances</u> was included. The national (federal) government had to share power with the states. The Senate had to share power with the House of Representatives. The president had to go to the Senate to approve treaties and confirm his cabinet appointees. Judges in federal courts are appointed by the president and confirmed by the Senate, but they have the power to make both behave. Judges are the referees who blow the whistle when anyone in government gets out of line.

A simple example of checks and balances is the passing of a law. Both the House and Senate must pass a bill in exactly the same form by a majority vote. It is then sent to the president. If the president signs it, it becomes a law; if the president doesn't like it, he (or she) vetoes it, and it goes back to Congress. After considering presidential objections,

Congress can pass it again, but it requires a two-thirds vote. What would keep the president from making a decision on a bill he didn't like and neither signing nor vetoing it? The Constitution gave him ten days (Sundays excluded) to either sign or veto. If the president does not act, it becomes law, unless Congress has adjourned, in which case, it does not become law (a pocket veto).

2. Separation of powers keeps the president from having too much influence over the workings of Congress and keeps Congress from intruding too much into the workings of the executive branch. The president has no power to remove a senator who complains about one of his policies, nor can the Congress fire the president or a cabinet member without going through the impeachment process for high crimes and misdemeanors. The Constitution does not allow either the president or Congress to interfere with decisions of the courts, and judges can only be forced from office through the impeachment process.

3. The federal government has control over foreign affairs, national security, and other policies requiring a national solution. It would have been very unwise to allow states to send diplomats and make separate deals with foreign countries. A national army and navy were needed for protection of the whole nation. Trade and commerce required a national currency (money) and rules regulating commerce between states. The need for national solutions has grown because of unforeseen changes. As long as a solution can be fit within the words of the Constitution, it is permitted by the courts. This is allowed because the "elastic clause" gives the power "to make all laws which shall be necessary and proper in carrying into execution the... powers" [listed in Article I, Section 8].

4. States are protected from the federal government. The Constitution provides that a state's boundaries cannot be moved without that state's consent. Governors and state legislatures answer to the people of their state, not to the president. As long as a state constitution or law does not violate the U.S. Constitution or national laws, it is valid. States still have great power to punish crimes, run schools and colleges, regulate businesses, build roads, set up their own systems of county and city governments, and operate state governments in their own ways.

5. It provides a system for peaceful change. The writers of the Constitution were not so arrogant as to assume they had solved every situation the nation might face, so they wisely devised a way to make change possible. The amendment system was included, but changes were not to be made without careful and slow consideration. An amendment requires a two-thirds vote of both houses and approval by three-fourths of the states. About 7,000 amendments have been proposed, but only 27 have survived the whole process.

Not all change has come because of amendments, however. Some change has come because courts have given new meaning to the words of the Constitution. Some phrases were vague enough for new advances in science and technology to be regulated by the federal government.

Name: ______________________________ Date: ________________

Questions

1. Can the House ignore the Senate and pass a bill on its own? YES/NO Why?

____

____

2. Who can veto a bill, and what happens to it after it is vetoed?

____

____

3. What majority is required by both houses of Congress to override the veto?

____

4. What is the general purpose of separation of powers?

____

____

5. What is the only way a president may be removed from office by Congress?

____

6. Can Alaska make a treaty with Russia? YES/NO Why?

____

____

7. What is another name for the "necessary and proper" clause of the Constitution?

____

8. Can the federal government move the boundary of your state and give the land to another state? YES/NO Why?

____

____

9. How large a majority is required in both houses of Congress to pass an amendment?

____

10. What percentage of states have to approve an amendment before it is ratified?

____

____

Organization of the Constitution and Amendments

The Constitution is divided into seven articles. Those are divided into sections. The basic format is:

Article I - The legislative branch
Article II - The executive branch
Article III - The judicial branch
Article IV - States
Article V - Amendment process
Article VI - Supremacy of the Constitution
Article VII - Ratification process

Amendments to the Constitution have been added to protect the rights of citizens, expand the numbers of those permitted to vote, allow the government to do something it could not otherwise do, or to improve something in the Constitution.

Amendments 1–10 Collectively known as the Bill of Rights.
Amendment 11 Protected states from outside lawsuits.
Amendment 12 Changed the presidential election process.
Amendments 13–15 Often called the Civil War amendments. They ended slavery, made the former slaves citizens, and allowed African-American men to vote.
Amendment 16 Permitted Congress to collect an income tax.
Amendment 17 Senators were to be elected by the people in the future.
Amendment 18 Prohibited the manufacture or sale of alcohol.
Amendment 19 Permitted women to vote.
Amendment 20 Moved up the date the president enters office and provided a method for replacing a president who died before taking office.
Amendment 21 Repealed the 18th Amendment.
Amendment 22 Limited a president to 10 years or 2 terms.
Amendment 23 Permitted citizens in the District of Columbia to vote for president.
Amendment 24 Abolished the poll tax that was required in a few states.
Amendment 25 Provided for a vacancy in the presidency and a method of choosing a new vice president after the former vice president became president.
Amendment 26 Allowed 18-year-olds to vote.
Amendment 27 Prohibited Congress from raising its pay until after the next election took place.

Article I, Sections 1–6

SECTION 1. The legislative branch consists of a Senate and House of Representatives.

SECTION 2, Paragraph 1. Members of the House are chosen every two years; a person eligible to vote for the lower house of the state legislature is qualified to vote for a candidate for the U.S. House.

Paragraph 2. To be a representative, a person must be at least 25 years old, a U.S. citizen at least seven years, and live in the state from which he (she) is elected.

Paragraph 3. Delete.

Paragraph 4. Vacancies in the House of Representatives must be filled by election. The governor issues the call for a new election.

Paragraph 5. The House chooses its own Speaker and has the power to impeach. *Impeachment means to bring charges that the person has committed a serious offense (discussed later in the Constitution). They are then tried in the Senate.*

SECTION 3, Paragraph 1. Each state is entitled to two senators chosen for six years; each senator has one vote.

Paragraph 2. Senators are divided into three classes, so one-third of the Senate is up for re-election every two years. Delete the last clause.

Paragraph 3. A senator must be at least 30 years old, a U.S. citizen at least nine years, and must reside in the state which elects him (her).

Paragraph 4. The vice president of the United States presides over the Senate, but can only vote if there is a tie. *As presiding officer of the Senate, the vice president is referred to as the President of the Senate.*

Paragraph 5. Other than the vice president of the United States, the Senate chooses its own officers; the Senate's presiding officer in the absence of the vice president is the President pro-tempore (temporary president).

Paragraph 6. The Senate tries all impeachment cases. Before the trial begins, they take an oath *to provide fair and impartial judgment.* If the president of the United States is on trial, the Chief Justice of the Supreme Court presides. No one can be found guilty unless two-thirds of the senators present vote for conviction.

Paragraph 7. A person found guilty by the Senate is removed from office and may not hold any office in the future in the federal government. The person found guilty may not be punished further by Congress, but is subject to trial, judgment, and punishment in a court.

SECTION 4, Paragraph 1. States will set the time, places, and rules for choosing candidates for Congress unless Congress sets the rules. *Congress has set the uniform date for general elections as the second Tuesday in November.*

Paragraph 2. Congress is to assemble at least once each year.

SECTION 5, Paragraph 1. Each house determines whether a member has been properly elected. A quorum consists of a majority of members; if there are less, they may adjourn, but those present may vote to penalize absent members.

Paragraph 2. Each house sets its own rules, punishes misbehavior, and a member may be removed by a two-thirds vote of that house's members.

Paragraph 3. Each house must keep a public record of its proceedings, except where they think secrecy is required. If as few as one-fifth of those voting feel that a vote yea or nay (yes or no) should be required, that vote must become part of the public record.

Paragraph 4. Neither house may adjourn for more than three days without the consent of the other house, nor may it hold its sessions in any other place than where the other is located.

SECTION 6, Paragraph 1. Members of Congress are paid out of the Treasury of the United States. They may not be tried (except for treason, felony [a major crime], or breach of the peace *[for example: drunk and disorderly behavior]*) while Congress is in session. They cannot be sued for anything they say in a speech or debate on the floor of their house.

Paragraph 2. No member of Congress can be appointed to any federal office during his (her) term. No one can be a member of Congress who holds some other office in the federal government.

Points to Consider in Article I, Sections 1–6

1. Congress has *two* houses, the House of Representatives and Senate.

2. The House of Representatives is limited to two-year terms. They wanted the House to be aware that they answered to the voters.

3. The requirements for the House were lower than for the Senate. The minimum age of 25 in the House was set there so Jonathan Dayton, 26, one of the members of the Convention, could be eligible.

4. Senators were to be chosen for six-year terms, and since they were chosen by the legislature, they were less responsive to public pressures. With higher requirements for office, it was assumed the Senate would be more proper in their behavior than the House.

5. The removal of the president, vice president, or other officers of the executive and judicial branches requires impeachment by the House and a trial by the Senate. Under all circumstances except the impeachment of the president, the vice president presides. Why doesn't he preside when the president is on trial? Because he might be tempted to help get the president removed so he could move up.

6. The writers made it difficult, but not impossible, for Congress to keep its sessions secret. That way the public stays informed on what Congress is doing.

7. Being paid by the U.S. Treasury reminds members of Congress they are working for all the people, not just the state the member represents.

Name: ______________________________ Date: ____________________

Open Book Pre-Test On Article I, Sections 1–6

Each of the following statements would violate some provision of Article I. You are to give the section and paragraph that has been violated.

Example:

The House of Representatives decides to give itself a big raise, but doesn't want to get bad publicity. They decide to keep their vote secret.

Article I, Section _5_ Paragraph _3_

1. After a member of the House dies, the governor appoints a replacement.

   Article I, Section ____ Paragraph ____

2. A 22-year-old is elected to the House of Representatives.

   Article I, Section ____ Paragraph ____

3. The president decides that the nation has too many laws already, so he orders Congress not to meet next year.

   Article I, Section ____ Paragraph ____

4. The president needs the vote of Senator Jones to get one of his projects through. He appoints Jones as ambassador to France, and Jones will receive both his Senate pay and a salary as ambassador.

   Article I, Section ____ Paragraph ____

5. To prevent Jones from voting against his project, the president orders the F.B.I. to arrest him on his way to the Senate, and put him in jail until after the vote is taken.

   Article I, Section ____ Paragraph ____

6. For his unconstitutional actions in the Jones matter, the president is impeached and fined $5,000 by the House.

   Article I, Section ____ Paragraph ____

7. At the president's Senate trial, the vice president presides.

   Article I, Section ____ Paragraph ____

8. Sixty senators vote for removal of the president, and 40 vote against removal. The president is ordered to leave the White House, and the vice president takes over.

   Article I, Section ____ Paragraph ____

Article I, Sections 7–10

SECTION 7, Paragraph 1. Tax bills originate in the House, but the Senate may approve or make changes as it can with other bills. *When there are disagreements between the two houses, a conference committee made up of members from both houses works out a compromise.* The bill must pass both houses in exactly the same form before it is sent to the president.

Paragraph 2. Bills approved by the House and Senate must go to the president before they can become law. If the president approves, he signs it; if he does not, he sends it back with his objections to the house where it originated *(in other words, he has vetoed it).* The house where it originated enters his objections in its record. After reconsidering it, if that house passes it by a two-thirds vote, it goes to the other house; if it passes by a two-thirds vote there, it becomes law. All votes to override the president's objections must be recorded with the names of those voting "yes" and "no" listed. The president must veto the bill within ten days (not counting Sundays) after it is sent to him, or it becomes law without his signature, *unless* Congress has adjourned. In that case, it is not a law *(this is called a "pocket veto").*

Paragraph 3. Whether Congress calls it a bill, order, or resolution, if it is passed by both houses, it must go to the president for approval (except in the case of adjournment). Before it goes into effect, it must be approved by the president, or Congress must override his objections by a two-thirds vote before it goes into effect.

SECTION 8. NOTE: This section lists (enumerates) the kinds of laws Congress can and cannot pass.

Paragraph 1. Congress has the power to tax imports and goods *(for example: a tax on cigarettes)*, pay the debts, and provide for the defense and general welfare of the United States; all taxes must be the same everywhere in the United States.

Paragraph 2. Congress has the power to borrow money and to regulate foreign trade, trade between states (interstate commerce), and trade with the Indian tribes. *This has been greatly expanded and includes the power to regulate TV stations, cyberspace, and airlines, among other things.*

Paragraph 3. Congress sets up rules for naturalization (the process by which those not born in the United States can become citizens) and rules for bankruptcies.

Paragraph 4. Congress has the power to coin money and regulate its value, to set the value of foreign money, and fix standards of weights and measures. *This includes such things as how much does a pound weigh and how long is an inch.*

Paragraph 5. Congress has the power to punish counterfeiters of securities (bonds, stock certificates, etc.) and money.

Paragraph 6. Congress has the power to establish post offices and roads over which mail is carried.

Paragraph 7. Congress has the power to promote science and practical arts by providing patents and copyrights to authors and inventors.

Paragraph 8. Congress has the power to create federal courts *(for example: district courts and courts of appeal)* inferior to the Supreme Court (which is specifically mentioned in Article III).

Paragraph 9. Congress defines and punishes piracy and crimes on the ocean and actions violating international law.

Paragraph 10. Congress has the power to declare war, commission privateers (privately owned ships allowed to raid enemy ships), and make rules for captures on land and ocean.

Paragraph 11. Congress has the power to raise and support armies; army appropriations are limited to no longer than two years. *This was to prevent the president as commander-in-chief from having money for his army over a longer time without answering to Congress.*

Paragraph 12. Congress has the power to provide and support a navy. *Notice there is no time limit; the reason is that it took a long time to build naval ships in those days.*

Paragraph 13. Congress has the power to make rules for the land and sea forces. *The president is commander-in-chief, but Congress makes the rules by which the armed forces are governed, a good example of checks and balances.*

Paragraph 14. Congress is to provide the rules for calling up the militia to execute the laws of the land, put down rebellions, and fight off invaders. *The militia has been replaced by the National Guard and Reserves; these are called up by the president under the system set up by Congress.*

Paragraph 15. Congress has the power to organize, arm, and discipline the militia and for making their rules while they are in federal service; the states have the authority to appoint militia officers and train the militia within the rules Congress has laid down.

Paragraph 16. Congress is to exercise control over a district (no larger than 10 miles square) that may be carved out of their lands by permission of the states where the district will be located. In similar fashion, lands given by the states for such purposes as building forts, gun powder magazines, arsenals, dockyards, and all other needed buildings will be controlled by rules set by Congress.

Paragraph 17. Congress may pass whatever laws are necessary and proper to carry out all of these listed powers and all other powers given by the Constitution to the government of the United States or its officials.

SECTION 9, Paragraph 1. Delete.

Paragraph 2. The only basis for taking away the privilege of a writ of habeas corpus will be in cases of rebellion or invasion where the public safety may require it. *Habeas corpus (ha-be-us cor-pus) is an important protection which requires that an accused person be brought before a judge and have the charges read to him. Without that right, one would never know why one was being held and could not prepare a defense against the accusations.*

Paragraph 3. Congress cannot pass a bill of attainder or an ex post facto law. *Bills of attainder are to punish only one person or a small group of individuals and convict them without a trial. Example: An airline pilot named Smith fell asleep and his plane crashed. Congress cannot vote to fine or imprison Pilot Smith for negligence. If a law passed provided that any pilot in the future whose plane crashed while he was asleep would be fined and sentenced to prison, that would not be a bill of attainder since it would apply to all pilots in the future.*

Ex post facto means a person cannot be fined or imprisoned for something he did before *the law was passed. In Pilot Smith's case, if Congress passed the law after his accident, he could not then be brought to court because of what he had done before it was passed. If he repeated the same thing, he could be brought to court for the second offense, but not the first one.*

Paragraph 4. Delete.

Paragraph 5. Congress cannot tax exports (goods leaving the country).

Paragraph 6. Import taxes will be the same at every port, and ships leaving one U.S. port cannot be required to stop at another U.S. port.

Paragraph 7. No money can be withdrawn from the treasury without an appropriation by Congress, and receipts and expenditures of all public money are to be published from time to time.

Paragraph 8. The United States cannot grant a title of nobility, and no official can, without the consent of Congress, accept any present, gift, office, or title from any king, prince, or foreign government. *Government officials are allowed to receive presents worth less than $50 from foreign governments since they are not likely to be "bribed" by the gift. More expensive gifts become the property of the U.S. government.*

SECTION 10, Paragraph 1. A state cannot enter a treaty or alliance with another nation, grant permission to raid enemy shipping, coin money or bills of credit (a substitute for money), substitute anything else for gold and silver as a way to pay debts, pass a bill of attainder, ex post facto law, or a law interfering with the obligation of contracts, or grant a title of nobility.

Paragraph 2. No state, unless it has the consent of Congress, may put a tax on imports or exports, except what may be necessary for enforcing inspection laws. Revenues from such inspection laws go to the U.S. Treasury, and Congress shall have the power to revise and control such laws.

Paragraph 3. No state, unless it has the consent of Congress, may tax ships, keep troops or armed ships in time of peace, enter an agreement with another state or a foreign nation, or engage in war unless it is invaded or in such danger of attack as will not allow delay.

Points to Consider in Article I, Sections 7–10

1. Since the House of Representatives was the "people's house" and was most sensitive to the wishes of the people, it was decided the House should be the place where taxing began.

2. It requires a simple majority to pass a bill, but a two-thirds vote in both houses to override the president's veto. In the vote to override the veto, it must be done with each member voting on the record. This provision suggests that the delegates thought the president's opinion was of great importance and that it must be considered.

3. The delegates showed some distrust of the president when they allowed him only ten days (Sundays excepted) to sign a bill. Otherwise, if the president did not like the bill and thought he would be overridden on a veto, he might do nothing with it and kill it. The exception was if Congress adjourned in the meantime. Since there was no place for the president to send the bill, he was permitted to do nothing with it (put it in his back pocket). This method of killing a bill is called a "pocket veto."

4. The delegates did not trust Congress either and did not allow Congress to pass any order or resolution that might be a sneaky substitute for an act without getting the president's approval.

5. The taxes listed did not include an income tax. The income tax was not constitutional until after the 16th Amendment was ratified.

6. Writers and inventors are protected by copyrights and patents which encourages creative efforts.

7. The National Guard (outgrowth of the earlier militia system) may be used by a state in case of disasters or riots. When the state National Guard units are not at the call of the president, the states' governors may use them when needed.

8. The District of Columbia was created out of land ceded by Maryland and Virginia and is ten miles square.

9. The "necessary and proper," or elastic clause, greatly increased the powers of the federal government. For example, it allowed Congress to create a Department of the Air Force without a constitutional amendment. If Congress has the authority to create an army and navy for the nation's defense, then it is logical it can create an air force for the same purpose.

10. The writ of habeas corpus was suspended in some areas by order of President Lincoln during the Civil War.

11. All of Article I describes what Congress can and cannot do, except for Section 10, which limits what states can do. Section 10 prevents states from making their own foreign policy and discourages them from interfering with trade by passing inspection laws. Whatever money is collected by inspections goes to the federal treasury, not the state treasury, and the costs of inspection are paid by the state.

Name: ______________________________ Date: ____________________

Open Book Pre-Test on Article I, Sections 7–10

The following bills are before Congress. Decide which of them are clearly constitutional and which are not. After circling "yes" or "no" (constitutional or unconstitutional), give the clause of the Constitution you use to justify your answer.

Example:

The president is given the title of Duke of Windtower by the Queen of England.

YES/(NO) Article I, Section *9* Paragraph *8*

1. Mr. Williams is arrested for cloning parakeets in 1995 for violating the anti-cloning law passed by Congress in 1998.

   YES/NO Article I, Section____ Paragraph____

2. Congress passes a law sentencing convicted counterfeiters to 20 years in prison.

   YES/NO Article I, Section____ Paragraph____

3. A bill the president has vetoed is passed over his veto by a vote of 300–135 in the House and 75–20 in the Senate and is declared a law.

   YES/NO Article I, Section____ Paragraph____

4. Congress passes a law punishing soldiers and sailors for theft on board ships and at military bases.

   YES/NO Article I, Section____ Paragraph____

5. Congress passes a law taxing cotton being exported to England.

   YES/NO Article I, Section____ Paragraph____

6. Texas puts a 10% import tax of its own on tomatoes grown in Mexico.

   YES/NO Article I, Section____ Paragraph____

7. Congress decides that no train operating in interstate commerce may have over 100 cars.

   YES/NO Article I, Section____ Paragraph____

8. A bill to tax fruitcakes passes in the Senate, then the House, and is signed into law by the president.

   YES/NO Article I, Section____ Paragraph____

Article II, Section 1

SECTION I, Paragraph 1. The president is in charge of the executive branch and serves a four-year term. Like the vice president, who is chosen for the same term, he shall be elected as follows:

Paragraph 2. Each state appoints, in whatever way the legislature chooses, electors equal to the number of senators and representatives to which the state is entitled in the Congress. No member of Congress or federal employee shall be chosen as an elector. *This Electoral College meets only once, and for only one purpose—to select the president and vice president. If a state has five representatives and two senators, it is entitled to choose seven electors. In practice, each political party chooses these seven electors in case it wins. If Party B's candidate wins the election, Party B's electors cast all seven votes; Party A's electors do not vote. This is often referred to as "winner takes all."*

Paragraph 3. Delete.

Paragraph 4. Congress will determine the date for choosing electors and the day on which they will vote. It will be the same date throughout the United States. *That date has been set as the first Tuesday after the first Monday in November.*

Paragraph 5. To be eligible for the office of president, a person must be a natural born (born in the United States or of U.S. citizens) citizen; the President must be at least 35 years old and have lived in the United States for 14 years.

Paragraph 6. Delete.

Paragraph 7. The president is to receive a salary which cannot be increased or decreased during the period for which he has been elected. He shall not receive during that period any compensation or special benefits from the United States or any state. *This keeps the president from being bribed by Congress or a state to approve something they want done.*

Paragraph 8. Before entering his duties as president, he takes the following oath or affirmation (this permitted Quakers and others who refuse to take oaths for religious reasons to take the oath without moral concern)—

"I do solemnly swear (or affirm) that I will faithfully execute the Office of the President of the United States, and will to the best of my ability, preserve, protect, and defend the Constitution of the United States."

Points to Consider in Article II, Section 1

1. The executive branch of the U.S. government is by far the largest of the three branches. It has the most employees doing the widest variety of jobs. It is much larger than anyone in 1787 could have ever dreamed. To put three million employees under one person would have been impossible if President Washington had not developed a cabinet system. In his time, there were only three executive departments (State, War, and Treasury). The system has expanded, but the idea is still the same. Each cabinet member answers to the president for his or her department, and the president has the power to fire the department head when he or she is not doing the job to satisfy him.

2. Giving the president enough power to be independent of Congress in doing his job yet keeping him from having too much power and ruling as some English kings had, was a serious problem for the Convention. They remembered how King Charles I had disbanded Parliament, and a civil war was fought to regain Parliament's control. They decided the later problems with King George III (sending armies to the colonies, taxing them without asking their consent, housing troops in people's homes, and taking away the authority of legislatures) must never happen again. In more modern words, they did not want to create a monster.

3. How was the president to be chosen? This was a hot topic. Many thought Congress should choose him, but others kept pointing out that the president would become a puppet on the string of Congress and could not be truly independent. That would not make separation of powers possible. A few thought the people should choose the president directly, but Roger Sherman doubted that the public would ever be well informed enough to make a good choice. In desperation, the Convention came to the Electoral College as a method for choosing the president. The Electoral College was based on the number of representatives and senators. It was accepted by the big states, which had more representatives than the smaller states, so they would have a greater influence in the selection of the president. Since the small states had the same number of senators, they had a larger percentage of electors than they had in percentage of population.

Remember that when voters cast ballots in the presidential election, they are choosing electors, and when a candidate gets a majority of electoral votes, he is the winner.

4. How long should the president serve, and should he have only one term? Some wanted the president to have the job during good behavior (in effect, life). Some wanted an eight-, 15-, or 30-year term, and at one point, a seven-year term was seriously considered. In the end, they decided on a four-year term with the president eligible for re-election.

5. The president cannot receive a higher or lower salary than what he is paid from the beginning of his term. The pay cannot be increased until after the next election. This keeps Congress from threatening the president with a pay cut if he does not go along with them or offering a pay raise if he will agree to approve some bill they have passed.

6. Notice that nothing is said about the vice president's responsibilities. John Adams, the first vice president, presided over the Senate, but the Senators did not let him take part in debate. Except for voting in the case of a tie, the vice president has often been ignored. In recent years, presidents have given them more jobs to do, and the vice president often goes to events when the president does not choose to go or cannot go.

7. Every president since Washington has taken the same oath of office. It is a reminder to them that their responsibility is to "preserve, protect, and defend the Constitution" and not to be popular or go along with anything Congress wants.

Name: ______________________________ Date: __________________

Open Book Pre-Test on Article II, Section 1

Decide which of the following statements are constitutional (yes) or unconstitutional (no). Give the paragraph in Article II, Section 1 that supports your answer.

Example:

Texas casts its vote for president on November 9 and New Hampshire on November 11.

YES/NO (circled) Article II, Section 1, Paragraph _4_

1. The president is elected to a six-year term.

   YES/NO Article II, Section 1, Paragraph ____

2. Smith was born of U.S. parents in 1940, and lived in the United States from 1940 to 1948. Then his father became a branch manager for a U.S. firm in Chile where Smith went to school and college. Smith returned to the United States in 1980. Was he eligible to run for president in the 1990 election?

   YES/NO Article II, Section 1, Paragraph ____

3. Congress gives the president a cost-of-living raise.

   YES/NO Article II, Section 1, Paragraph ____

4. A member of the U.S. Senate is chosen as an elector.

   YES/NO Article II, Section 1, Paragraph ____

5. Was a person born in 1953 eligible to be president in the 1992 election?

   YES/NO Article II, Section 1, Paragraph ____

6. A state with eight representatives casts ten electoral votes.

   YES/NO Article II, Section 1, Paragraph ____

7. New York electors cast their vote for president two days ahead of the electors from Hawaii.

   YES/NO Article II, Section 1, Paragraph ____

8. A state wishes to present a house to the former president.

   YES/NO Article II, Section 1, Paragraph ____

Article II, Sections 2–4

SECTION 2, Paragraph 1. The president is commander-in-chief of the army and navy of the United States, and of the militia when called into the service of the United States. He may require in writing from his cabinet and other public officials of the executive departments reports on any subject related to their departments. He has the power to grant reprieves and pardons for any crime against the United States except in cases of impeachment.

As commander-in-chief, the president appoints generals and admirals with the consent of the Senate. However, only Congress can declare war, and all funds to pay the expenses of the army and navy must first be appropriated by Congress, and it is Congress that sets the rules by which the army and navy live. In criminal matters, the name for these rules is the Uniform Code of Military Justice. The president's authority over the military is far from complete, and they are not his private army and navy. This prevents him from using them to threaten Congress. Usually, the militia (now National Guard) are not in federal service, but is under the control of the state's governor. That command shifts when the president calls the units into federal service.

In his role as chief executive, the cabinet and other officers of the federal government answer to the president, and many top officials can be fired by him at any time. Indirectly, Congress also has much influence on these officials. It is Congress that confirms many of them, and Congress appropriates the money for their departments. Department officials are often called before Congressional committees to explain their policies.

The president has the power to grant reprieves or pardons. A reprieve may save someone from execution, but the person will serve prison time instead. A pardon frees the person from serving prison time. A well-known use of the pardon was President Ford's pardon of former President Nixon for any violations of law he might have committed while he was president. For obvious reasons, the president cannot pardon a person impeached; otherwise, he might forgive himself or a close friend in the executive branch.

Paragraph 2. The president has the power to make treaties, which do not become effective unless two-thirds of the Senate concur. With the advice and consent of the Senate, he appoints ambassadors, other public ministers and consuls, judges of the Supreme Court, and all other officers of the United States which shall be established by law. Congress may decide to allow less important officials to be chosen by the president, the courts, or by heads of departments.

The treaty-making provision makes the president the chief diplomat of the United States. In this role, he gets information and advice from a wide variety of sources including diplomats, military intelligence, the Central Intelligence Agency, and the National Security Council. Treaties must be approved by a two-thirds vote of the Senate before they are in effect.

Ambassadors are sent to represent the nation in relations with foreign governments; consuls protect the interests of citizens doing business and traveling in foreign countries. Justices of the Supreme Court and judges in other federal courts are appointed by the president but must be confirmed (approved) by the Senate.

Rather than send every employee of the federal government through the long and difficult confirming process, the writers of the Constitution wisely left it up to Congress to decide which officials were important enough to require such approval.

Paragraph 3. If the Senate is in recess (and therefore cannot confirm the president's nominee for a vacant post), the president may appoint someone temporarily; their right to hold office will expire at the end of the next session of Congress.

If the ambassador to Russia resigns, the president needs and has the authority to put someone in that job temporarily; it cannot wait for a later time.

SECTION 3, Paragraph 1. From time to time the president is to give Congress information on the State of the Union and recommend policies he may consider needed and useful. Under unusual circumstances, he may call Congress, or one of the houses of Congress, into special session. If the two houses are in disagreement over the time of adjournment, he may adjourn them for such a time as he thinks proper. He will receive foreign ambassadors and other public officials. He will see that the laws are faithfully executed, and commissions all officers of the United States.

The State of the Union does not require a speech to a joint session of Congress as is done today. President Jefferson was a poor public speaker, so he started sending a written message instead. That continued until President Wilson revived the speech method again in 1913. The president uses the speech as a way to emphasize things he considers important and any bills he thinks should be passed by Congress.

Congress is rarely called into special session. President Lincoln did not even call Congress back at the beginning of the Civil War. The possibility that circumstances may require a meeting of Congress is provided for.

Since the two houses of Congress are equal, a disagreement between them over adjournment has to be decided by someone; the Constitution gives that "tie-breaker" role to the president.

Receiving and sending ambassadors is a more important role than many might assume. If the president does not approve of the policies of a certain country and refuses to accept an ambassador from that country, the United States does not have diplomatic relations with them. The United States did not have diplomatic relations with Russia from 1917 to 1933, for example.

The president becomes the "chief executive" because he sees that laws are faithfully executed.

SECTION 4. The president, vice president, and all other officers of the United States may be removed from office by impeachment and conviction of treason, bribery, or other high crimes and misdemeanors.

The process of impeachment and trial is spelled out in Article I of the Constitution. Grounds for impeachment and removal are given in Article II. Treason is an attempt to overthrow your own government or betraying its best interests through dealings with a foreign government. Bribery is receiving money or some valuable gift that influences one's policies. High crimes and misdemeanors are violations of law of a serious nature.

Only one president, Andrew Johnson, came close to being removed from office for "high crimes." Charges against President Clinton brought an impeachment, but fell far short of the two-thirds needed to convict in the Senate. Former Vice President Aaron Burr was tried in federal court for treason, but since he no longer held federal office, he could not be impeached. Several federal judges and cabinet members have been impeached and removed from office.

Points to Consider in Article II, Sections 2–4

1. A major responsibility for the president is national defense. If he does everything else well and fails to protect the nation, he is a failure. With the United States playing the most important role of any nation around the globe, the United States is often involved in peace-keeping efforts in far-off places.

2. The power to make treaties and send and receive ambassadors is an important part of the president's job. There have been times when the president's treaty was rejected by the Senate, which was very embarrassing for him. The most important of those occasions was the Senate's rejection of President Wilson's Treaty of Versailles after World War I. It is usually wise for the president to keep the Senate informed and supportive during the treaty-making process so the Senate does not reject the treaty once it is completed. It is another reminder of the checks and balances of the U.S. government.

3. The appointment of Supreme Court justices is important for many years beyond the president's term. Chief Justice John Marshall was appointed by President John Adams and served long after Adams and his Federalist party were dead. President Franklin Roosevelt was so angry with the conservatives on the Supreme Court he proposed adding more members to the Court. This was called "court-packing" and was rejected by large numbers in both the House and Senate.

4. The process for impeaching a president or vice president is difficult for a very good reason. It keeps Congress from removing a president for petty reasons, such as disagreeing with them on policies, or removing a president who belongs to the other party.

Name: ______________________________ Date: __________________

Open Book Pre-Test on Article II, Sections 2–4

Decide which of the following statements are constitutional (yes) or unconstitutional (no). Give the section and paragraph in Article II that supports your answer.

Example:

The president orders the Secretary of Defense to explain in writing why he has not provided enough ammunition to troops in the field.

(YES)/NO Article II, Section _2_ Paragraph _1_

1. The president fires the Secretary of Defense.

   YES/NO Article II, Section ___ Paragraph ___

2. The treaty signed by the president and passed by the Senate by a 60–40 vote is declared U.S. national policy.

   YES/NO Article II, Section ___ Paragraph ___

3. The president uses the State of the Union address to focus on the need for better roads and bridges.

   YES/NO Article II, Section ___ Paragraph ___

4. The House decides to impeach the vice president for accepting a bribe.

   YES/NO Article II, Section ___ Paragraph ___

5. The Senate replaces a retiring federal judge with Mr. Smith over the president's objections.

   YES/NO Article II, Section ___ Paragraph ___

6. The president decides to reprieve a federal prisoner facing the death sentence.

   YES/NO Article II, Section ___ Paragraph ___

7. Despite tensions between the United States and Shurkestan, the president receives the Shurkestani ambassador.

   YES/NO Article II, Section ___ Paragraph ___

8. The murder of the Speaker of the House by order of the president results in the president's impeachment and removal from office.

   YES/NO Article II, Section ___ Paragraph ___

Article III

<u>SECTION I.</u> Judicial power of the United States is vested in the Supreme Court and other courts that Congress may create. Judges in all federal courts will hold their offices during good behavior and shall receive salaries on a regular basis; these salaries cannot be cut. *The Supreme Court is the only one specifically mentioned in the Constitution and has existed since President Washington appointed the first justices. The Constitution does not say how many justices will be on the Supreme Court, and the number has varied from six to ten. For many years, there have been nine justices on the Supreme Court. When vacancies occur, the president appoints a new justice with the Senate's consent.*

There are a large number of "inferior" courts, including courts of appeal, district courts, tax courts, bankruptcy courts, and so on. A person dissatisfied with a verdict in a lower court may appeal to a higher court, but the final word in all such cases is a decision by the U.S. Supreme Court.

<u>SECTION 2, Paragraph 1.</u> The judicial power of federal courts shall include all cases arising under the Constitution, the laws and treaties made by the United States to all cases involving ambassadors, other public officials, and consuls; to all cases involving naval and maritime supervision; to controversies in which the United States is a party; to controversies between two or more states;(—Delete—between citizens of different states), and between a state or one of its citizens and foreign governments and their citizens or subjects.

Wherever the federal government is involved, federal courts have jurisdiction (the power to decide). That may seem to give the federal government the upper hand, but remember that federal judges are beyond control by the president or Congress, and their salaries cannot be cut if they rule against the federal government.

Giving federal courts control over ambassadors, other public officials, and consuls is included because their cases are often complicated by treaty obligations and international law.

Giving federal courts control over admiralty (naval) and maritime (civilian shipping) is included because these cases are often outside any state's limits. A case of a merchant ship accidently damaging a naval ship would be a good example of this type of case.

Controversies between two or more states are settled in federal court because a court in State A cannot enforce its will on State B.

<u>Paragraph 2.</u> In all cases involving ambassadors, other public officials, consuls, and those in which a state is a party, the Supreme Court has original jurisdiction (the Supreme Court is the first to hear the case). In all other cases previously mentioned, the Supreme Court has appellate jurisdiction (cases may be appealed to it) unless Congress makes different rules.

The power of the Supreme Court to hear cases on appeal has been expanded because the 14th Amendment has made many actions by states and state courts subject to review in federal courts.

Paragraph 3. Except in cases of impeachment, trial in federal courts will be by jury, and the trial will take place in the state where the crime was committed, but when not committed within a state, the trial may be anywhere that Congress may, by some law, have directed.

This was to prevent the government from moving a trial from Florida, where there were witnesses who might help the defendant, to Alaska where they might not be willing or able to go. In cases of crime at sea or in the air where state jurisdiction might be doubtful, federal courts decide these cases.

SECTION 3, Paragraph 1. Treason against the United States is limited to making war against the United States, switching to the enemy side, or aiding or helping the enemy. No person can be convicted of treason without two witnesses to the same open or unconcealed action or without confessing to the crime in open court.

Treason is the most serious crime against a nation, but charges of treason were often used by kings who wanted to take someone's property or destroy a critic. The Constitution limited conviction for treason to a small list of actions: making war against the United States or helping an enemy. It made conviction difficult as well. Two witnesses to the defendant's actions or the defendant confessing guilt in a courtroom with witnesses present are needed for conviction.

Paragraph 2. Congress shall have the power to set the punishment for treason, but that punishment may not include punishment for members of the family who were not involved in the crime, and any property seized must be returned to the heirs after the traitor's death.

The punishment for treason is limited to the one found guilty, but cannot punish those who were simply related to the convicted person. This prevents the government from declaring people guilty to steal their land and other property. Whatever is taken has to be returned to the heirs.

Points to Consider in Article III

1. Federal judges serve during "good behavior" and, once appointed, can only be removed by impeachment. They have no masters. For example, even though President Nixon had appointed three justices to the Supreme Court himself, he lost by 9–0 in the Supreme Court when it ordered him to turn the Watergate tapes over to the independent counsel.

2. The role of federal courts has increased greatly over the years, and while the public sometimes disagrees with their decisions, they have been good examples of fairness and justice. In part, that is due to their lack of fear that Congress will punish them by lowering their pay.

Name: ________________________________ Date: ____________________

Open Book Pre-Test on Article III

Decide which of the following statements are constitutional (mark yes), and which are unconstitutional (mark no). Give the section and paragraph in Article III that support your answer.

Example:

A case where a citizen sues the federal government is tried in state court.

YES/NO (NO circled) Article III, Section *2* Paragraph *1*

1. The English ambassador is tried for a parking violation in a Maryland court.

   YES/NO Article III, Section____ Paragraph____

2. The president is angered by a federal district judge's decision in a case and fires him.

   YES/NO Article III, Section____ Paragraph____

3. Without the defendant giving up (waiving) his rights, a federal judge decides to try him without a jury.

   YES/NO Article III, Section____ Paragraph____

4. An armed robbery is committed on a U.S. registered cruise liner between the United States and the Bahamas. The defendant is tried in U.S. district court.

   YES/NO Article III, Section____ Paragraph____

5. Congress decides to cut the pay of federal judges by ten percent.

   YES/NO Article III, Section____ Paragraph____

6. While the United States is at war, Mr. Evil is caught selling missile information to the enemy country and is tried in federal court for treason.

   YES/NO Article III, Section____ Paragraph____

7. Three witnesses are brought before the court who witnessed the exchange of missile information, and Mr. Evil was found guilty.

   YES/NO Article III, Section____ Paragraph____

8. After Mr. Evil's trial, he is hanged and his property is seized. After the execution, the government will not return the property to the heirs.

   YES/NO Article III, Section____ Paragraph____

Articles IV–VII (4 through 7)

Article IV, SECTION 1. Each state is to give full acceptance of the laws and judicial proceedings of other states. Congress may by law develop a process by which this takes place. *When a person is found guilty in one state of a crime, they cannot escape punishment by fleeing to another state. A driver's license issued in one state is valid in the other states.*

SECTION 2, Paragraph 1. Citizens of one state are entitled to all rights of citizens in other states. *When traveling in another state, you have the same rights as citizens of that state have.*

Paragraph 2. A person escaping justice from State A who is captured in State B is to be returned to State A after the governor of State A requests his return. *This is called extradition. It is usually done, but there have been situations where the fugitive has not been returned.*

Paragraph 3. Delete.

SECTION 3, Paragraph 1. New states may be created by Congress, but they cannot be formed by putting two existing states together or taking land away from a state without the consent of the legislature of the state or states and by the approval of Congress.

Paragraph 2. Congress has the power to sell or make rules and regulations for the territories or other properties of the United States. This is not to be construed as taking sides in disputes between the federal government and states. *Congress decides policy toward the territories like Puerto Rico, and, if it gives permission, they have a degree of self-rule. On the other hand, states do not need permission from Congress to pass their laws.*

SECTION 4. Congress will guarantee every state a representative government, will protect them from being invaded, and if the governor requests (at times when the legislature is not in session), it will be protected against rioters. *In practice, the governor requests that the president send troops to put down a riot.*

Article V. Amendments may be proposed by two methods: (1) By a two-thirds vote of both Houses of Congress, or (2) If two-thirds of state legislatures call for a convention for proposing amendments. The proposed amendment must then be approved by three-fourths of state legislatures or by conventions in three-fourths of the states. No state, without its permission, shall be deprived of equal representation in the Senate.

The amendments allow a peaceful means of changing the Constitution but are difficult to pass. This keeps popular but bad ideas from becoming part of the Constitution.

Article VI, Paragraph 1. Debts of the United States incurred during the Confederation period are valid obligations of the federal government.

Paragraph 2. The Constitution and the laws and treaties made by the United States to carry out its provisions are the supreme law of the land. Judges in any state are bound to abide by its provisions in their rulings regardless of any provision in state law that conflicts with it. *This is often referred to as the "Supremacy Clause" of the Constitution. It makes the Constitution, and all federal laws and treaties, more important than the state constitutions or laws.*

Paragraph 3. All members of Congress, all members of state legislatures, and all officers of the executive and judicial branches of the federal or state governments are to swear by oath or affirmation to support this Constitution. No religious test shall ever be required as a qualification for any federal office. *Whether the person is elected as U.S. Senator or as county judge, the person must swear to uphold the Constitution of the United States. A person does not have to be a Christian or believe in God to hold federal office. At the time the Constitution was written, many states did require a statement that the officeholder was a Christian, but that requirement was dropped later by all states.*

Article VII. Ratification (approval) of the Constitution by conventions in nine states was sufficient for it to go into effect in those approving states. *Notice that they did not send it to state legislatures where it would have probably failed to be ratified, because states were giving up control over some important rights they had always enjoyed.*

Points to Consider in Articles IV–VII

1. Article IV was included to protect the authority of states and their courts in providing a system for returning fugitives and making sure their decisions were carried out. The escape of a fugitive is too easy in modern times for states to control without that provision.

2. Article V allows for changes in the Constitution, but makes the process slow. It is often years between a proposal being approved in one house of Congress and its final approval by three-fourths of the states. On some amendments, you may notice that Congress provided it must be approved in seven years.

3. The Supremacy Clause in Article VI brought state constitutions, laws, governors, legislators, and all public officials in line to uphold and defend the U.S. Constitution. Despite many differences that still exist in state laws, they all must conform to the Constitution, laws, and treaties of the United States.

4. The ratification provision in Article VII faced great difficulty in some states. New York ratified it by a bare majority of 30-27. At the time Washington was inaugurated as the first president, two states were still outside the Union: North Carolina and Rhode Island. When they realized that being outside made business and dealings with other states difficult if not impossible, they caved in and approved.

The main argument used by critics of the Constitution (labeled Anti-Federalists) was that it had no bill of rights. James Madison promised that when Congress assembled, that would be corrected, and it was.

Name: ______________________ Date: ______________

Open Book Pre-Test on Articles IV–VII

Decide which of the following are constitutional (mark yes) and which are unconstitutional (mark no). Give the article, section, and paragraph that support your answer. If there is only one section, answer Section 1, and only one paragraph, answer Paragraph 1.

Example:
Congress decides to set up a government in a new territory.

(YES)/NO Article *IV* Section *3* Paragraph *2*

1. New York will not provide legal counsel to a poor person from Illinois even though they provide free legal counsel to their own poor.

   YES/NO Article _____ Section _____ Paragraph _____

2. A California judge ignores federal law and says he is responsible only to California law.

   YES/NO Article _____ Section _____ Paragraph _____

3. Congress decides that Rhode Island is too small and should be united with Massachusetts. Rhode Island agrees to become an ex-state.

   YES/NO Article _____ Section _____ Paragraph _____

4. Forty state legislatures demand that a convention be called to require a balanced federal budget. Congress refuses to act.

   YES/NO Article _____ Section _____ Paragraph _____

5. An escapee from an Idaho prison is captured in Wyoming. After a request from Idaho's governor, the Wyoming governor sends him back.

   YES/NO Article _____ Section _____ Paragraph _____

6. The House refuses to seat Muhammed Altabar only on the basis that he is not a Christian.

   YES/NO Article _____ Section _____ Paragraph _____

7. Oregon passes a law regarding whaling that ignores a U.S. treaty. Can it be enforced?

   YES/NO Article _____ Section _____ Paragraph _____

8. Michigan refuses to recognize a Wisconsin driver's license as valid.

   YES/NO Article _____ Section _____ Paragraph _____

Amendments 1–5

True to his word, James Madison delivered on his promise to provide a bill of rights to the U.S. Constitution shortly after Congress convened. The first ten amendments were passed by Congress in 1789 and ratified by three-fourths of the states in 1791. There are some things to keep in mind about the Bill of Rights.

1. No right can be carried to an extreme. You cannot deliberately lie about someone and claim you are protected by free speech. You cannot declare yourself a church and claim that your salary is protected from taxes by the freedom of religion. You cannot gather in the middle of the night on someone's lawn with a boom box blaring and claim freedom of assembly.

2. Courts have defined and redefined rights until they are very confusing. Everything you need to know in understanding what is and what is not legal is far beyond the ability of this material to cover. Only a few basics of what courts have said for several years will be included.

3. The Bill of Rights was written to control what the federal government could do. It was not until after the passing of the 14th amendment that it limited what states could do. Some rights (for example: a jury trial) that limit federal actions do not restrict states.

4. Some amendments are hotly debated, and only a brief glimpse into these amendments is included. Much more information is available on the Internet or in written sources to support each side.

Amendment 1. Congress may not establish a religion or prohibit the right to exercise one's religious beliefs, limit freedom of speech, of the press, the right of peaceable assembly, or prohibit complaining by petition to government about its actions.

An "established church" was a national church supported by tax money. Religious beliefs are one thing; actions are another. A person may believe his religion allows him to rob banks, but that belief will not save him from going to prison if he acts on it.

Freedom of speech and press may also be limited if they create a danger to public safety, health, or morals. Peaceable assembly may require a permit, and limits may be set on when and where to keep streets and buildings open for the public's use. The right to petition keeps public officials from refusing to listen to citizen complaints.

Amendment 2. Since a well-regulated militia is necessary for the security of a free nation, the right of the people to keep and bear arms shall not be limited.

Few issues will create as much debate as this one. The ANTI-GUN supporters say that the right is based on the need in the eighteenth century for militia; since that need has disappeared, strong restrictions on guns are needed to curb violence. The PRO-GUN supporters say that with few exceptions, the person has the right to keep and carry arms, and the rights of law-abiding citizens cannot be limited.

Amendment 3. In times of peace, troops cannot be quartered in private homes without the owner's consent, nor can it be done in wartime except in a manner set by law.

This was included because British troops were housed in private homes in the pre-Revolutionary period and during the war, and homeowners could do nothing to stop them.

Amendment 4. The people's right to have security for their own bodies and in their houses shall not be violated; papers and belongings are protected against unreasonable searches and seizures. No search warrants may be issued without probable cause supported by oath or statement. The warrant must describe the place to be searched and the persons or things to be captured or seized.

The old saying, "A man's home is his castle," is the basis for this limit on government. The people well remembered when British troops carried warrants (writs of assistance) allowing them to search anywhere for anything and used those warrants to harass patriots. The search warrant today requires specific information about who is being searched for and what evidence the police are seeking to find.

Amendment 5. No person can be brought to trial for a capital or other major offense without a grand jury bringing an indictment or written charges. The exception is in cases involving the army, navy, or militia when in service during war or public danger. No person will be subject to double jeopardy (being brought to trial twice) for the same offense, and cannot be forced in a criminal trial to be a witness against himself. No person can be executed, imprisoned, or property seized without due (formal) process of law; private property cannot be taken without just compensation.

A grand jury hears evidence and decides whether there are enough facts to support bringing an accused person to court. Those in military service do not have the same protection, but are under the Uniform Code of Military Justice. Those in the military receive some, but not all, rights of civilians.

The "double jeopardy" provision is to keep government from harassing the citizen by constantly taking him to court for the same crime. It does not protect him from being brought to trial for different offenses of which he has been accused. If he has kidnapped someone and taken them across state lines, he might be tried for taking a kidnapped person across state lines in federal court and for kidnapping in state courts.

A person does not testify in federal or state courts if he or she is the defendant. If he or she wants to testify, however, he or she can. Due process is following the rules, and unless that is done, the defendant cannot be punished. Taking a person's property for a public purpose cannot be done without giving a fair price for that property.

Name: ______________________________ Date: ____________________

Open Book Pre-Test on Amendments 1–5

State which of the first five amendments would be argued in court in each of these circumstances.

1. A student newspaper is shut down after publishing its critical remarks of rules set down by the Board of Education.

   Amendment ________

2. A witness is told he must give testimony in court even though giving it could implicate him in the crime.

   Amendment ________

3. The government offers to pay $10,000 for land worth $50,000.

   Amendment ________

4. Congress debates a law requiring all guns to be registered.

   Amendment ________

5. Outside the Pentagon, police break up a crowd chanting and carrying placards protesting military involvement somewhere.

   Amendment ________

6. Because of overcrowded conditions at a barracks, the army orders homeowners near the base to make rooms available for soldiers.

   Amendment ________

7. In their search for a stolen car, police search a suspect's kitchen drawers.

   Amendment ________

8. Congress decides that any man, regardless of his conscience, may be required to serve in the armed forces during a war.

   Amendment ________

Amendments 6–12

The purpose of the Bill of Rights was to make sure government did not abuse its power. In Amendment 4, we saw limits on how evidence was to be gathered; in Amendment 5, we saw limits on trials (the defendant did not have to testify in court, he could not be tried twice for the same offense, and could not be convicted without proper trial). In Amendments 6 and 8, we see more protections for the accused. The fear of powerful government taking liberty away from the people was more important than the protection of society from the law violator.

Amendment 6. The accused is entitled to a speedy trial in an open court; he is to be tried in the state and district where the crime was committed; he has the right to know the charges made against him, to confront the witnesses testifying against him, to require testimony from witnesses who can testify for him, and to have legal counsel for his defense.

If a defendant is held too long before trial, it is like serving prison time, so limits are set from the time of arrest until the trial takes place. If the defendant keeps the trial from being heard by legal maneuvers, he cannot claim he was denied a speedy trial. Trials are to take place in the state and district where the crime took place. The defendant has the right to cross-examine witnesses, to issue subpoenas requiring witnesses to testify for him, and to have attorneys for his defense.

Amendment 7. In civil suits where the amount disputed is over $20, the parties have a right to trial by jury; any appeal of the jury's ruling must be judged by common law rules.

The rights in criminal matters had already been covered. This amendment involves non-criminal situations where the issue is usually damages. The parties may choose to have the judge rather than a jury settle the issue. This amendment does not carry over to state courts which have their own rules regarding juries.

Amendment 8. Excessive bail cannot be required; excessive fines cannot be imposed; cruel and unusual punishments cannot be inflicted.

Bail is a pledge of money or property guaranteeing the accused will appear in court. This depends on the nature of the offense, the evidence against the accused, the financial ability of the accused, and the character of the accused. "Cruel and unusual" outlaws torture and slow death.

Amendment 9. The person has other rights that might not have been listed.

In other words, not every right may have been included, but that does not mean an American has lost them.

Amendment 10. The states and citizens of the states have not lost their rights just because they have not been included.

The 9th and 10th Amendments were inserted to make sure the federal government did not take away a freedom just because it was not mentioned.

Amendment 11. (Adopted in 1798) A state cannot be sued by citizens of another state or foreigners.

This was to prevent states from being sued without their permission.

Amendment 12. (Adopted in 1804) *The writers of the Constitution did not have a crystal ball and did not predict the coming of political parties. Under the original Constitution, electors cast two votes (for president and vice president). The candidate with the most votes became president, and the one with the second-highest number became vice president. By 1800, political parties developed, and the candidate for president (Jefferson) had exactly the same number of electoral votes as the vice presidential candidate Burr. Following the procedure required by Article II, Section 1, Paragraph 3 of the Constitution, the election went to the House where Jefferson was chosen president, but obviously this situation should not be repeated. This explanation will help explain why Amendment 12 was needed and approved before the next election took place.*

Electors were now to cast separate ballots for president and vice president. If no candidate for president received a majority of votes, the House was to choose the president from the top three candidates; each state would cast one vote. If no vice presidential candidate received a majority of electoral votes, the Senate would choose from the top two candidates. If a president was not chosen by March 4 (Inauguration Day), the vice president was to serve as president until the choice was made. A person not eligible to be president was not eligible to be vice president.

Despite many criticisms of using electoral votes rather than having a popular election of the president, the system has worked well with the exceptions of the 1824 election (with four candidates receiving electoral votes, the House chose J.Q. Adams) and the 1876 election (where election returns were questioned because of violence in three states).

Before the Civil War, twelve amendments had been ratified: the first ten (the Bill of Rights) to protect individual and state liberties, the eleventh to protect states from being sued, and the twelfth to correct an unexpected defect in the original Constitution.

Name: ______________________________ Date: ____________________

Open Book Pre-Test on Amendments 6–12

State which of the amendments would be argued in court in each of these circumstances.

1. Despite protests from the defendant, a federal judge decides to hear a $1 million lawsuit without a jury.

   Amendment _______

2. The presidential candidate coming in fourth in the Electoral College receives the vote of a state delegation in the House.

   Amendment _______

3. Bond is set at $1 million for an accused jaywalker.

   Amendment _______

4. A person protests that even though the right to privacy is not listed in the Constitution, it is a right he still has.

   Amendment _______

5. Arrested in 1994 for murder, the accused is still waiting for his trial despite his wish to get it over with.

   Amendment _______

6. The day of the inauguration has arrived, and no president has been chosen. The vice president becomes president until the selection has been made.

   Amendment _______

7. The defendant's attorney is not allowed to cross-examine a prosecution witness.

   Amendment _______

8. A person is found guilty of assault and sentenced to 100 lashes.

   Amendment _______

Amendments 13–15 (The Civil War Amendments)

The Constitution had not solved two big issues. One was whether the African-American was a citizen entitled the rights to life, liberty, and property. In 1857, the Supreme Court ruled in *Dred Scott vs. Sandford* that African-Americans were not citizens with full protection of the Constitution. Correcting that decision was a basis for the 14th Amendment.

A second issue was whether a state that felt its rights were being denied could leave the Union. After years of arguing, eleven Southern states left the Union and formed the Confederate States of America in 1860–1861, and the Civil War followed. The war answered the second question, but it took legal remedies to cure the first issue. This led to passage of the so-called Civil War amendments discussed in this section.

Amendment 13. (Adopted in 1865). *The famous Emancipation Proclamation had applied only to those states and areas still fighting against the United States on January 1, 1863; it did not include states and areas then under U.S. control. This amendment was needed to expand its provisions to all regions of the nation.*

SECTION 1. Slavery and other forms of involuntary labor, except as punishment for crime, shall not exist in the United States or in any place controlled by the United States.

SECTION 2. Congress shall pass appropriate laws to carry out the amendment.

Notice that this amendment applied to both the federal and state governments. Incidentally, the drafting of men for military service does not violate this amendment since they are not slaves.

Amendment 14. (Adopted in 1868). *The 13th Amendment ended slavery, but had not given African-Americans national or state citizenship. Southern states passed laws limiting African-Americans but not restricting whites. The 14th Amendment was passed to give African-Americans the protection of citizenship. Parts of Sections 2 and 3 are not discussed because they are no longer relevant.*

SECTION 1. All born or naturalized in the United States and subject to its authority are citizens of the United States and of the state where they reside. No state can make or enforce laws that take away the rights and privileges of citizens of the United States. No state may take away from any person their life, liberty, or property without fair processes, nor deny equal protection of the law to anyone within its boundaries.

SECTION 2. For purposes of representation in the House, everyone in the state will count as a person except untaxed Indians. If male U.S. citizens over 21 are denied the vote for electors for president and vice president, that state's representation in Congress shall be reduced proportionally.

This was intended to make sure Southern states allowed African-American males to vote. If the state did not, they were threatened with losing power in the House. That threat was never carried out.

SECTION 3. Delete

SECTION 4. The public debt of the United States, including future debts caused by pensions and bounties during the war, is valid. The Confederate war debt, or state debts incurred in fighting the war, is not valid.

SECTION 5. Congress has the power to enforce the provisions by appropriate laws.

The importance of the 14th Amendment's Section 1 was not felt at first, but became important when Bill of Rights freedoms were used to protect citizens from state actions. When states threaten a citizen's freedom of speech, those rights are as protected as they would be if the federal government were doing it.

Amendment 15. (Adopted in 1870)

SECTION 1. No citizen can be denied the right to vote because of race, color, or because he had been a slave.

SECTION 2. Congress has the power to enforce the provisions by appropriate laws.

The 15th Amendment was passed because Southern states were not allowing the former slaves to vote. States could still legally control the right to vote with residence requirements or literacy tests as long as they did not discriminate against African-American males.

By about 1900, Southern states found many ways to keep African-American men from voting with unfair literacy tests, poll taxes, making the Democratic party a white-only political club, and threatening any black man who dared to vote. This led to segregation, and African-Americans lost rights they were not able to regain until the 1950s and 1960s.

Points to Consider in Amendments 13–15

1. The Civil War was a very important four years in American history, and it caused many changes. Before the war, northern blacks were not allowed to do many things whites could do. Some states made it illegal for them to live in that state. They could not vote in most states. The 14th and 15th Amendments had some effect on African-Americans in the North.

2. The main effect was on the South. Freeing slaves and giving former slaves the right to vote was a major change that white Southerners did not like, and it caused great racial tension for many years to come. In the 1950s and 1960s, African-Americans began to demand those rights they had lost during the time of Jim Crow (segregation) laws.

Name: ______________________________ Date: ____________________

Open Book Pre-Test on Amendments 13–15

Imagine yourself an African-American male in 1872. State which part of the Civil War amendments affect you in each of the following situations.

1. Your former master would not let you leave his land.

   Amendment ________

2. You went to the polls and voted for the first time.

   Amendment ________

3. Your state passed laws affecting only African-Americans.

   Amendment ________

4. Your former master refused to pay wages to black workers.

   Amendment ________

5. Your state decided to give compensation to citizens who bought Confederate bonds.

   Amendment ________

6. You were denied the right to attend the theater because of your race.

   Amendment ________

7. You could not vote because a person of another race threatened to kill you if you did.

   Amendment ________

8. A state law requires that you ride on a separate street car for blacks only.

   Amendment ________

Amendments 16–21

By 1900, many Americans were looking at their nation, and while they were sure it was the greatest nation on the planet, they also saw problems that needed fixing: the rich not paying their share of the cost of government, forests and wildlife being destroyed, corruption in government, children working in factories instead of going to school, alcohol damaging families, and the need for better schools and recreation. Reformers called Progressives began to work to improve America. Four amendments to the Constitution were a direct result of their concerns (the 16th, 17th, 18th, and 19th Amendments). The 20th and 21st Amendments were added in 1933 and had the effect of shortening the time between election and inauguration and ending prohibition.

Amendment 16. (Adopted in 1913) Congress has the power to lay and collect taxes on incomes without any regard for census.

The federal government had relied mostly on tariffs and land sales to pay its expenses. The first income tax was levied in 1913 and now is the major source of government revenues.

Amendment 17. (Adopted in 1913) Paragraph 1. Each state will have two senators elected by the people for six years, and each senator will have one vote. A person eligible to vote for the largest branch of the state legislature can vote for senators.

Paragraph 2. When vacancies occur, the governor of the state will issue an election notice to fill the vacancy; however, the state legislature may give the governor the authority to make temporary appointments until the election when the people will choose a senator.

Paragraph 3. Delete.

The major change made here was that senators were to be chosen by the people, not the legislature. The amendment resulted from increasing charges of corruption in the Senate, and a desire to make the senators answer to the public, not to the legislature.

Amendment 18. (Adopted in 1919). Delete.

This amendment prohibited the manufacturing, selling, or transporting of intoxicating liquors within the United States and its territories. It was repealed by the 21st Amendment in 1933.

Amendment 19. (Adopted in 1920). Paragraph 1. Women may not be denied the right to vote.

Paragraph 2. Congress has the power to enforce this amendment by legislation.

Some states had already given women the right to vote, but this amendment gave all women the vote. It was the result of a long struggle on the part of the women's suffrage movement that had started in 1848.

In 1932, the nation was in the Great Depression. President Hoover had been voted out of office in November, but President Roosevelt could not take office until March 4. Neither the outgoing nor incoming president could do much except wait until inauguration day. The time lag required in 1787 was no longer necessary, and it could be dangerous. That led to the quick passage and adoption of the 20th Amendment.

Amendment 20. (Adopted in 1933). SECTION 1. The terms of president and vice president will end at noon on January 20, and the terms of senators and representatives at noon on January 3 of the years in which their terms would end if this article had not been ratified. Their successors' terms begin when theirs end.

SECTION 2. Congress is to assemble at least once a year; that meeting will begin on January 3 unless Congress chooses a different date.

SECTION 3. If the president-elect shall have died before January 20, the vice president-elect becomes president. If a president shall not have been chosen by January 20 or if the president-elect fails to be qualified, the vice president-elect shall act as president until the president is qualified. Congress may by law provide for a case where neither the president-elect nor vice president-elect qualifies, declaring who will act as president, and that person shall act until the president-elect or vice president-elect shall have qualified.

SECTION 4. Congress may provide for the case of death where the person the House of Representatives has selected is unable to fulfill the office and the death of the person the Senate has designated as vice president.

SECTION 5. Delete.

SECTION 6. Delete.

The main effect of the 20th Amendment is to move up the date of the inauguration from March to January; the only reasons a president or vice president might not qualify are that they do not meet the constitutional requirements (very unlikely) or that the House and Senate have to do the choosing and have not completed the work by January 20 (also unlikely). The main purpose of Sections 3 and 4 is to provide a system that insures that a president is ready to take office on January 20 under any circumstance.

Amendment 21. (Adopted in 1933). Paragraph 1. This amendment repeals the 18th Amendment.

Paragraph 2. The transporting or importing of liquor into any state that chooses to continue prohibiting liquor is prohibited.

Paragraph 3. Delete.

Name: ______________________________ Date: ____________________

Open Book Pre-Test on Amendments 16–21

State which amendment was passed to solve each of the problems listed below.

1. Women were not allowed to vote, and many thought that was unfair.

   Amendment _______

2. The Senate did not answer to the voters, but only to the state legislature.

   Amendment _______

3. The rich should be paying more of the tax burden than they have in the past.

   Amendment _______

4. There are too many drunks in this country.

   Amendment _______

5. What if the president-elect dies before the inauguration?

   Amendment _______

6. The prohibition amendment is not working as people thought it would.

   Amendment _______

7. What happens if a senator dies or resigns?

   Amendment _______

8. When would be a better time than March for the new president to be inaugurated?

   Amendment _______

Amendments 22–27

Six amendments have been added since World War II. Some are short, but Amendment 25 is long and complicated.

Amendment 22. (Adopted in 1951) Paragraph 1. No person can be elected president more than twice, and no one who has acted as president more than two years can be elected more than once.

Paragraph 1. Delete.

President Franklin Roosevelt had been elected four times, and many Americans felt that should not be repeated. In the future, no president was to serve more than ten years.

Amendment 23. (Adopted in 1961). SECTION 1, Paragraph 1. The District of Columbia was to appoint by a method Congress may direct:

Paragraph 2. Electors for president and vice president equal to the number of electors no more than the least populated state. They shall meet in the District and perform their duties.

SECTION 2. Congress has the power to enforce this amendment.

The Constitution had never provided a way for those who lived in the District of Columbia to vote for president. This amendment corrected that situation. Notice that it did not give them representation in Congress. They are now allowed a non-voting delegate to the U.S. House.

Amendment 24. (Adopted in 1964). The right to vote for president and vice president, or for U.S. senator and representative in Congress, shall not be denied because the person has failed to pay a poll tax or other tax.

Some Southern states required a person to pay the poll tax before that person could vote. Collected several months before the election, it was a method of keeping the poor from voting.

Note: A number of concerns came together to create the 25th Amendment. One worry was that in the modern age, only the president had the authority to take the necessary steps in case of a nuclear attack. Suppose he or she was unable to do this? It could possibly happen. President Garfield had been disabled several months before he died, President Wilson suffered a stroke, President Eisenhower had heart attacks, and President Kennedy would have faced a long recovery period if he had survived the assassination in 1963.

The possibility that a president might suffer some physical or emotional breakdown that would create a danger to the nation and the world was also a concern, so a system to relieve the president of his powers might be needed.

Another concern was the lack of a vice president when the former vice president became president. This had happened after the recent deaths of Presidents Franklin Roosevelt and John Kennedy.

Amendment 25. (Adopted in 1967). SECTION 1. If the president is removed, dies, or resigns, the vice president becomes president.

SECTION 2. Whenever there is no vice president, the president will nominate a vice president who shall take office after he has been confirmed by the U.S. Senate and House.

SECTION 3. When the president informs the President pro tempore of the Senate and Speaker of the House in writing that he is unable to discharge the duties of his office, those duties shall be carried out by the vice president until the president informs the President pro tempore and Speaker that he is able to carry out his duties.

SECTION 4. Paragraph 1. If the vice president and a majority of the cabinet or some other group Congress may provide, inform the President pro tempore of the Senate and Speaker of the House in a written statement that the president is unable to carry out the powers and duties of his office, the vice president shall immediately assume his powers of Acting President.

Paragraph 2. When the president informs the President pro tempore and the Speaker in writing that no inability exists, he again resumes his office unless the vice president and a majority of the cabinet, or other body designated by law, inform the President pro tempore and the Speaker in writing that the president is unable to assume his responsibilities.

Congress will decide the issue, assembling within 48 hours for that purpose if it is not already in session. Congress has 21 days after receiving the vice president and cabinet's statement or 21 days after they are required to assemble to settle the issue. It will take a two-thirds vote of both Houses to decide that the president is unable to carry out his responsibilities; if that standard is met, the vice president will continue to serve as Acting President. Without a two-thirds majority in both houses, the president resumes the responsibilities of his office.

Amendment 26. (Adopted in1971). SECTION 1. The right of citizens over the age of 18 years to vote shall not be denied on account of age.

SECTION 2. Congress shall have the power to enforce this amendment.
The idea was that if a young man can be drafted, he should be able to vote.

Amendment 27. (Adopted in 1992). Salaries for members of Congress cannot be changed until after the next election of representatives has occurred.

This amendment was added to prevent Congress members from raising their salaries over taxpayer objections.

Name: ______________________________ Date: ____________________

Open Book Pre-Test on Amendments 22–27

State which amendment was passed to solve each of the problems listed below.

1. Young adults complaining that they are being denied the right to vote.

   Amendment ________

2. Poor people complaining they cannot vote because of the poll tax.

   Amendment ________

3. The nation needs to have a vice president who can take over if the president dies.

   Amendment ________

4. If everyone else can vote for president, why can't the people in the nation's capital?

   Amendment ________

5. If Congress raises its salary, no one can stop them.

   Amendment ________

6. A popular president might continue getting elected until he begins to think of himself as a king.

   Amendment ________

7. What happens if a president becomes mentally ill, and begins behaving strangely?

   Amendment ________

8. What is the fair way to deal with the situation when a vice president has served only a small part of the former president's term; should he be permitted to be elected to a second term as president?

   Amendment ________

Name: ______________________________ Date: ____________________

Missing Words From the Constitution

The following quotes from the Constitution come with key words missing. If you have studied the Constitution carefully, you may remember them without looking them up. Go through the quotes, and see how many you can fill in without looking them up. If you can answer 13 of the 15, you will do very well on the Constitution test. If you can answer 11 of the 15, you remember enough that you should pass it. If you can answer less than half, go over the Constitution carefully; you have not studied it enough and may not do well on the test.

Preamble. We the people of the United States, in order to form a more perfect _____...

1. ____________________

Preamble. Establish justice, insure domestic tranquility, provide for the common _____ and promote the general welfare...

2. ____________________

Article I. All legislative powers herein granted shall be vested in a _____ of the United States.

3. ____________________

Article I. No person shall be a representative who shall not have attained to the age of twenty-five years, and been _____ years a citizen of the United States.

4. ____________________

Article I. The _____ of the United States shall be President of the Senate...

5. ____________________

Article I. The _____ shall have the sole power to try all impeachments...

6. ____________________

Article I. All bills for raising revenue shall originate in the _____...

7. ____________________

Article I. [Congress shall have the power] to raise and support armies, but no appropriation of money to that use shall be for a longer term than _____ years.

8. ____________________

Article II. The _____ power shall be vested in a President of the United States.

9. ____________________

Article II. The president shall be _____ of the Army and Navy of the United States...

10. ____________________

Name: ______________________________ Date: ____________________

Article II. He [the president] shall from time to time give to the Congress information of the ______.

11. ______________________________

Article III. The judicial power of the United States shall be vested in one ______, and in such inferior courts as the Congress may ... ordain and establish.

12. ______________________________

Article IV. The United States shall guarantee to every state in this Union a ______ form of government...

13. ______________________________

Article V. The Congress, whenever ______ of both houses shall deem it necessary, shall propose Amendments to this Constitution...

14. ______________________________

Article VI. This Constitution and the laws of the United States which shall be made in pursuance thereof; and all treaties made, or which shall be made, under the authority of the United States, shall be the ______ law of the land...

15. ______________________________

Memory Check

If the president, a senator, and a representative are talking, and each of them barely reaches the minimum age for their office, what is their combined age?

1. ______________________________

The 100 senators vote in an impeachment trial. How many must vote for removal before the official is removed?

2. ______________________________

The 435 members of the House of Representatives all vote on a bill. How many must vote in favor before it is passed?

3. ______________________________

Name: ______________________________ Date: ____________________

Missing Words From the Amendments

The following quotes from amendments to the Constitution come with key words missing. See how many blanks you can fill in without looking in the amendments for answers. If you can answer seven or eight without looking them up, you should do very well on the Constitution test. If you can answer five or six, you remember enough to pass it. If you cannot answer at least four, you have not studied well enough and may do poorly on the test.

Amendment 1. Congress shall make no law respecting an establishment of ______...

1. ______________________

Amendment 4. The right of the people to be secure in their persons, houses, papers, and effects, against unreasonable ______ and seizures...

2. ______________________

Amendment 6. In all criminal prosecutions, the accused shall enjoy the right to a ______ and public trial...

3. ______________________

Amendment 8. Excessive ______ shall not be required, nor excessive fines imposed...

4. ______________________

Amendment 13. Neither ______ nor involuntary servitude, except as punishment...

5. ______________________

Amendment 20. The terms of the president and vice president shall end at noon on the 20th day of______...

6. ______________________

Amendment 22. No person shall be elected to the office of president more than ______...

7. ______________________

Amendment 26. The right of citizens of the United States, who are ______ years of age or older...

8. ______________________

Name: ______________________________ Date: ____________________

Constitution Test

Section 1: Background for the Constitution. Place the letter of the term that best fits the description on the line beside the description.

_____ 1. Colonial governors were usually appointed by the ________.

_____ 2. The upper house of a colonial legislature

_____ 3. Author of the Articles of Confederation

_____ 4. Leader of the rebellion closing Massachusetts courts

_____ 5. American negotiating the treaty unpopular with the West and South

_____ 6. Meeting where trade on the Potomac River was discussed

_____ 7. Meeting to discuss trade problems among the states

_____ 8. Presided at the Constitutional Convention

_____ 9. Youngest delegate to the Convention

_____ 10. New York delegate favoring a strong national government

_____ 11. Proposed the Great Compromise

_____ 12. Principle involved when Congress keeps the president from having too much power

_____ 13. Principle allowing each branch to do its job without too much interference from the others

_____ 14. Approval given by the states to the Constitution

_____ 15. Adding a new provision to the Constitution

A. Amendment
B. Annapolis
C. Checks and balances
D. Council
E. Dayton
F. Dickinson
G. Hamilton
H. Jay
I. King
J. Mount Vernon
K. Parliament
L. Ratification
M. Separation of powers
N. Shays
O. Sherman
P. Washington

Name: ________________________ Date: ________________

Section 2. If the statement is true, put a T in the T column; if it is false, put an F in the F column. Statements may refer to either the Constitution or amendments.

T F

__ __ 1. American governments (federal and state) all have four branches.

__ __ 2. Representation in both Houses of Congress is by population.

__ __ 3. The Constitution sets higher requirements to be a senator than to be a representative.

__ __ 4. Impeachment takes place in the House, the trial in the Senate.

__ __ 5. The "President pro tempore" is an officer in the House.

__ __ 6. A two-thirds vote in both houses is required to override a veto.

__ __ 7. Rules for the military are written by the president.

__ __ 8. Ex post facto laws punish someone for something they did before the law was passed and are unconstitutional.

__ __ 9. States cannot sign agreements with each other unless Congress has given permission.

__ __ 10. Amendment 1 freedoms include speech, press, and the right to own a gun.

__ __ 11. The vice president can only vote when there is a tie in the Senate.

__ __ 12. Treaties require a two-thirds vote in both houses of Congress.

__ __ 13. Only the president has the power to pardon a federal crime.

__ __ 14. Crimes on the high seas are tried in the courts of the nearest state.

__ __ 15. If a person is found guilty of treason, his innocent family members cannot be punished.

__ __ 16. Amendments must be approved by three-fourths of the states before they go into effect.

__ __ 17. The president has a major role in the amendment process.

__ __ 18. A person cannot be denied the right to vote if the only reason is that she is African-American or is 18-years old.

__ __ 19. Women were given the right to vote before African-Americans were.

__ __ 20. If a president is very ill, there is no way his powers may be given to the vice president.

Name: ______________________________ Date: ____________________

Section 3. Multiple Choice. On the line, put the letter of the answer that best completes the statement.

_____ 1. In order to qualify for the House of Representatives, a person must be at least how old?

A. 20 B. 25 C. 30.

_____ 2. The number of senators a state has is determined by:

A. population B. land size C. each state has two Senators.

_____ 3. The qualifications to be a representative are:

A. lower than for a senator B. higher than for a senator

C. the same as for a senator.

_____ 4. The listed power that is not given to Congress:

A. establish post offices B. tax exports C. declare war.

_____ 5. During his term in office, the president's salary may:

A. be raised but not lowered B. be lowered but not raised

C. not be changed.

_____ 6. The president is all the following except:

A. Commander-in-Chief B. head of executive branch

C. head of judicial branch.

_____ 7. The salary of a federal district judge:

A. may be raised but not lowered B. may be lowered but not raised

C. cannot be changed.

_____ 8. An amendment to the Constitution may be proposed by:

A. the president B. two-thirds of both houses

C. the Supreme Court.

_____ 9. Before it can go into effect, an amendment must be approved by:

A. the president B. the Supreme Court

C. three-fourths of states.

_____ 10. The Bill of Rights is:

A. in the original Constitution B. the first ten amendments

C. the first four amendments.

_____ 11. Amendment 1 includes all freedoms listed below except:

A. peaceful assembly B. press

C. no quartering of troops in homes.

Name: ______________________________ Date: ____________________

_____ 12. The amendment beginning "A well regulated militia" goes on to discuss:

A. right to bear arms B. military duties

C. protection of states from invasion.

_____ 13. A person "taking the fifth" is referring to protection from:

A. excessive bail B. testifying against himself C. double jeopardy.

_____ 14. According to Amendment 12, if no candidate for president has a majority of electoral votes:

A. the candidate with the most votes wins,

B. the House chooses from the top 3

C. a new election is held.

_____ 15. Amendment 13 (passed in 1865) abolished:

A. slavery B. the poll tax C. taxes on exports.

_____ 16. The first to get to vote were:

A. African-American men B. women

C. residents of the District of Columbia.

_____ 17. The last tax to be approved was the:

A. tax on imports B. tax on exports C. tax on income.

_____ 18. No one can be elected president:

A. more than once B. more than twice C. there are no limits.

_____ 19. Amendment 24 outlawed which tax?

A. poll B. income C. import.

_____ 20. Amendment 25 provides a system for replacing the:

A. Speaker B. vice president C. cabinet member.

Section 4. According to the Constitution and amendments, which of the following requires more than a simple majority? If more is required, place an M in the M column; if a simple majority is enough, place an S in the S column.

M S

__ __ 1. A treaty

__ __ 2. A bill

__ __ 3. Election by the Electoral College

__ __ 4. Confirmation by the Senate

__ __ 5. Trial for impeachment

Name: ______________________________ Date: ____________________

Section 5. Who is the only person who can make each of these statements accurately? Place the letter of the correct person on the line next to each statement.

_____ 1. I am the presiding officer of the Senate.

_____ 2. Most government employees work under me.

_____ 3. I hold the highest office in the House.

_____ 4. I preside when a president is on trial.

_____ 5. When a Senator dies, I can appoint someone to his post until the next election.

A. Chief Justice
B. Governor
C. President
D. Speaker
E. Vice president

Section 6. Sequence. Place the letter of the quotation in each group that appears first in the Constitution and amendments on the blank next to the group number.

_____ 1. A. We the people of the United States…
B. Each house shall be the judge of the elections…

_____ 2. A. All bills for raising revenue…
B. No person except a naturalized citizen…

_____ 3. A. The judicial power shall extend to all cases…
B. A well-regulated militia being necessary…

_____ 4. A. The Congress shall have the power to lay and collect taxes on incomes…
B. The terms of the president and vice president shall end at noon on the 20th day…

_____ 5. A. Excessive bail shall not be required…
B. The eighteenth article of amendment to the Constitution is hereby repealed…

Portraits of Delegates to the Constitutional Convention

Jonathan Dayton
New Jersey

John Dickinson
Delaware

Oliver Ellsworth
Connecticut

Benjamin Franklin
Pennsylvania

Elbridge Gerry
Massachusetts

Alexander Hamilton
New York

James Madison
Virginia

Luther Martin
Maryland

George Mason
Virginia

Portraits of Delegates to the Constitutional Convention

Gouverneur Morris
Pennsylvania

William Patterson
New Jersey

Charles Pinckney
South Carolina

Charles Cotesworth Pinckney
South Carolina

Edmund Randolph
Virginia

John Rutledge
South Carolina

Roger Sherman
Connecticut

George Washington
Virginia

James Wilson
Pennsylvania

The Constitution of the United States

(Italicized words indicate portions of the Constitution that are no longer in effect.)

Preamble
We the people of the United States, in Order to form a more perfect Union, establish Justice, insure domestic Tranquility, provide for the common defense, promote the general Welfare, and secure the Blessings of Liberty to ourselves and our Posterity, do ordain and establish this Constitution for the United States of America.

ARTICLE I ***(Legislature)***

Section 1. All legislative Powers herein granted shall be vested in a Congress of the United States, which shall consist of a Senate and House of Representatives.

(House of Representatives)
Section 2. The House of Representatives shall be composed of Members chosen every second Year by the People of the several States, and the Electors in each State shall have the Qualifications requisite for Electors of the most numerous Branch of the State Legislature.

(Qualifications for Representatives)
No Person shall be a Representative who shall not have attained to the Age of twenty five Years, and been seven Years a Citizen of the United States, and who shall not, when elected, be an Inhabitant of that State in which he shall be chosen.

(Method of Apportionment)
Representatives and direct Taxes shall be apportioned among the several States which may be included within this Union, according to their respective Numbers, *which shall be determined by adding to the whole Number of free Persons, including those bound to Service for a Term of Years, and excluding Indians not taxed, three fifths of all other Persons.* The actual Enumeration shall be made within three Years after the first Meeting of the Congress of the United States, and within every subsequent Term of ten Years, in such Manner as they shall by Law direct. The Number of Representatives shall not exceed one for every thirty Thousand, but each state shall have at Least one Representative; *and until such enumeration shall be made, the State of New Hampshire shall be entitled to choose three, Massachusetts eight, Rhode Island and Providence Plantations one, Connecticut five, New York six, New Jersey four, Pennsylvania eight, Delaware one, Maryland six, Virginia ten, North Carolina five, South Carolina five, and Georgia three.*

(Vacancies)
When vacancies happen in the Representation from any State, the Executive Authority thereof shall issue Writs of Election to fill such Vacancies.

(Rules of the House, Impeachment)
The House of Representatives shall choose their Speaker and other Officers; and shall have the sole Power of Impeachment.

(Senators)
Section 3. The Senate of the United States shall be composed of two Senators from each State, *chosen by the Legislature thereof,* for six Years; and each Senator shall have one Vote.

Immediately after they shall be assembled in Consequence of the first Election, they shall be divided as equally as may be into three Classes. The Seats of the Senators of the first Class shall be vacated at the Expiration of the second Year, of the second Class at the Expiration of the fourth Year, and of the third Class at the Expiration of the sixth Year, so that one third may be chosen every second Year; *and if Vacancies happen by Resignation, or otherwise, during the Recess of the Legislature of any State, the Executive thereof may make temporary Appointments until the next Meeting of the Legislature, which shall then fill such Vacancies.*

(Qualifications of Senators)
No Person shall be a Senator who shall not have attained to the Age of thirty Years, and

been nine Years a Citizen of the United States, and who shall not, when elected, be an Inhabitant of that State for which he shall be chosen.

(Vice President)

The Vice President of the United States shall be President of the Senate, but shall have no Vote, unless they be equally divided.

The Senate shall choose their other Officers, and also a President *pro tempore,* in the Absence of the Vice President, or when he shall exercise the Office of President of the United States.

(Impeachments)

The Senate shall have the sole Power to try all Impeachments. When sitting for that Purpose, they shall be on Oath or Affirmation. When the President of the United States is tried, the Chief Justice shall preside: And no Person shall be convicted without the Concurrence of two thirds of the Members present.

Judgment in Cases of Impeachment shall not extend further than to removal from Office, and disqualification to hold and enjoy any Office of honor, Trust or Profit under the United States: but the Party convicted shall nevertheless be liable and subject to Indictment, Trial, Judgment and Punishment, according to Law.

(Elections)

Section 4. The Times, Places and Manner of holding Elections for Senators and Representatives, shall be prescribed in each State by the Legislature thereof; but the Congress may at any time by Law make or alter such Regulations, except as to the places of choosing Senators.

(Sessions)

The Congress shall assemble at least once in every Year, and such Meeting *shall be on the first Monday in December, unless they shall by Law appoint a different Day.*

(Proceedings of the House and the Senate)

Section 5. Each House shall be the Judge of the Elections, Returns and Qualifications of its own Members, and a Majority of each shall constitute a Quorum to do Business; but a smaller Number may adjourn from day to day, and may be authorized to compel the Attendance of absent Members, in such Manner, and under such Penalties, as each House may provide.

Each House may determine the Rules of its Proceedings, punish its Members for disorderly Behavior, and, with the Concurrence of two thirds, expel a Member.

Each House shall keep a Journal of its Proceedings, and from time to time publish the same, excepting such Parts as may in their Judgment require Secrecy; and the Yeas and Nays of the Members of either House on any question shall, at the Desire of one fifth of those Present, be entered on the Journal.

Neither House, during the Session of Congress, shall, without the Consent of the other, adjourn for more than three days, nor to any other Place than that in which the two Houses shall be sitting.

(Members' Compensation and Privileges)

Section 6. The Senators and Representatives shall receive a Compensation for their Services, to be ascertained by Law, and paid out of the Treasury of the United States. They shall in all Cases, except Treason, Felony and Breach of the Peace, be privileged from Arrest during their Attendance at the Session of their respective Houses, and in going to and returning from the same; and for any Speech or Debate in either House, they shall not be questioned in any other Place.

No Senator or Representative shall, during the Time for which he was elected, be appointed to any civil Office under the Authority of the United States, which shall have been created, or the Emoluments whereof shall have been increased during such time; and no Person holding any Office under the United States, shall be a Member of either House during his Continuance in Office.

(Money Bills)

Section 7. All Bills for raising Revenue shall originate in the House of Representatives; but the Senate may propose or concur with Amendments as on other Bills.

(Presidential Veto and Congressional Power to Override)

Every Bill which shall have passed the House of Representatives and the Senate, shall, before it becomes a Law, be presented to the President of the United States; If he approves he shall sign it, but if not he shall return it, with his Objections to that House in which it shall have originated, who shall enter the Objections at large on their Journal, and proceed to reconsider it. If after such Reconsideration two thirds of that House shall agree to pass the Bill, it shall be sent, together with the Objections, to the other House, by which it shall likewise be reconsidered, and if approved by two thirds of that House, it shall become a Law. But in all such Cases the Votes of both Houses shall be determined by yeas and Nays, and the Names of the Persons voting for and against the Bill shall be entered on the Journal of each House respectively. If any Bill shall not be returned by the President within ten Days (Sundays excepted) after it shall have been presented to him, the Same shall be a Law, in like Manner as if he had signed it, unless the Congress by their Adjournment prevent its Return, in which Case it shall not be a Law.

Every Order, Resolution, or Vote to which the Concurrence of the Senate and House of Representatives may be necessary (except on a question of Adjournment) shall be presented to the President of the United States; and before the Same shall take Effect, shall be approved by him, or being disapproved by him, shall be repassed by two thirds of the Senate and House of Representatives, according to the Rules and Limitations prescribed in the Case of a Bill.

(Congressional Powers)

Section 8. The Congress shall have Power

To lay and collect Taxes, Duties, Imposts and Excises, to pay the Debts and provide for the common Defense and general Welfare of the United States; but all Duties, Imposts and Excises shall be uniform throughout the United States;

To borrow Money on the credit of the United States;

To regulate Commerce with foreign Nations, and among the several States, and with the Indian tribes;

To establish an uniform Rule of Naturalization, and uniform Laws on the subject of Bankruptcies throughout the United States;

To coin Money, regulate the Value thereof, and of foreign Coin, and fix the Standard of Weights and Measures;

To provide for the Punishment of counterfeiting the Securities and current Coin of the United States;

To establish Post Offices and post Roads;

To promote the Progress of Science and useful Arts, by securing for limited Times to Authors and Inventors the exclusive Right to their respective Writings and Discoveries;

To constitute Tribunals inferior to the supreme Court;

To define and punish Piracies and Felonies committed on the high Seas, and Offenses against the Law of Nations;

To declare War, grant Letters of Marque and Reprisal, and make Rules concerning Captures on Land and Water;

To raise and support Armies, but no Appropriation of Money to that Use shall be for a longer Term than two Years;

To provide and maintain a Navy;

To make Rules for the Government and Regulation of the land and naval Forces;

To provide for calling forth the Militia to execute the Laws of the Union, suppress Insurrections and repel Invasions;

To provide for organizing, arming, and disciplining, the Militia, and for governing such Part of them as may be employed in the Service of the United States, reserving to the States respectively the Appointment of the Officers, and the Authority of training the Militia according to the discipline prescribed by Congress;

To exercise exclusive Legislation in all Cases whatsoever, over such District (not exceeding ten Miles square) as may, by Cession of particular States, and the Acceptance of Congress, become the Seat of Government of the United States, and to exercise like Authority over all Places purchased by the Consent of the Legislature of the State in which the same shall be, for the Erection of Forts, Magazines, Arsenals, Dock-yards, and other needful Buildings;—And

To make all Laws which shall be necessary and proper for carrying into Execution the foregoing Powers, and all other Powers vested by this Constitution in the Government of the United States, or in any Department or Officer thereof.

(Limits on Congressional Power)

Section 9. *The Migration or Importation of such Persons as any of the States now existing shall think proper to admit, shall not be prohibited by the Congress prior to the Year one thousand eight hundred and eight; but a Tax or duty may be imposed on such Importation, not exceeding ten dollars for each Person.*

The Privilege of the Writ of Habeas Corpus shall not be suspended, unless when in cases of Rebellion or Invasion the public Safety may require it.

No Bill of Attainder or ex post facto Law shall be passed.

No Capitation, or other direct, Tax shall be laid, unless in Proportion to the Census or Enumeration herein before directed to be taken.

No Tax or Duty shall be laid on Articles exported from any State.

No Preference shall be given by any Regulation of Commerce or Revenue to the Ports of one State over those of another: nor shall Vessels bound to, or from, one State, be obliged to enter, clear, or pay Duties in another.

No Money shall be drawn from the Treasury, but in Consequence of Appropriations made by law; and a regular Statement and Account of the Receipts and Expenditures of all public Money shall be published from time to time.

No Title of Nobility shall be granted by the United States: And no Person holding any Office of Profit or Trust under them, shall, without the Consent of the Congress, accept of any present, Emolument, Office, or Title, of any kind whatever, from any King, Prince, or foreign State.

(Limits on Powers of the States)

Section 10. No State shall enter into any Treaty, Alliance, or Confederation; grant letters of Marque and Reprisal; coin Money, emit Bills of Credit; make any Thing but gold and silver Coin a Tender in Payment of Debts; pass any Bill of Attainder, ex post facto Law, or Law impairing the Obligation of Contracts, or grant any Title of Nobility.

No State shall, without the Consent of Congress, lay any Imposts or Duties on Imports or Exports, except what may be absolutely necessary for executing its inspection Laws: and the net Produce of all Duties and Imposts, laid by any State on Imports or Exports, shall be for the Use of the Treasury of the United States; and all such Laws shall be subject to the Revision and Control of the Congress.

No State shall, without the Consent of Congress, lay any Duty of Tonnage, keep Troops, or Ships of War in time of Peace, enter into any Agreement or Compact with another State, or with a foreign Power, or engage in War, unless actually invaded, or in such imminent Danger as will not admit of delay.

ARTICLE II ***(Executive)***

(President)

Section 1. The executive Power shall be vested in a President of the United States of America. He shall hold his Office during the Term of four Years, and, together with the Vice President, chosen for the same Term, be elected as follows

(Election of President)

Each State shall appoint, in such Manner as the Legislature thereof may direct, a Number of Electors, equal to the whole Number of Senators and Representatives to which the State may be entitled in the Congress: but no Senator or Representative, or Person holding an Office of Trust or Profit under the United States, shall be appointed an Elector.

(Electors)

The Electors shall meet in their respective States, and vote by Ballot for two Persons, of whom one at least shall not be an inhabitant of the same State with themselves. And they shall make a List of all the Persons voted for, and of the Number of Votes for each; which List they shall sign and certify, and transmit sealed to the Seat of Government of the United States, directed to the President of the Senate. The Presi-

dent of the Senate shall, in the Presence of the Senate and House of Representatives, open all the Certificates, and the votes shall then be counted. The Person having the greatest Number of Votes shall be the President, if such Number be a Majority of the whole Number of Electors appointed; and if there be more than one who have such Majority, and have an equal Number of votes, then the House of Representatives shall immediately choose by Ballot one of them for President; and if no Person have a Majority, then from the five highest on the List the said House shall in like Manner choose the President. But in choosing the President, the Votes shall be taken by States, the Representation from each State having one Vote; A quorum for this purpose shall consist of a Member or Members from two thirds of the States, and a Majority of all the States shall be necessary to a Choice. In every Case, after the Choice of the President, the Person having the greatest Number of Votes of the Electors shall be the Vice President. But if there should remain two or more who have equal votes, the Senate shall choose from them by Ballot the Vice President.

The Congress may determine the Time of choosing the Electors, and the day on which they shall give their Votes; which Day shall be the same throughout the United States.

(Qualifications of President)

No person except a natural born Citizen, *or a Citizen of the United States, at the time of the Adoption of this Constitution,* shall be eligible to the Office of President; neither shall any Person be eligible to that Office who shall not have attained to the Age of thirty five Years, and been fourteen Years a Resident within the United States.

(Succession to the Presidency)

In Case of the removal of the President from Office, or of his Death, Resignation, or Inability to discharge the Powers and Duties of the said Office, the Same shall devolve on the Vice President, and the Congress may by Law provide for the Case of Removal, Death, Resignation, or Inability, both of the President and Vice President, declaring what Officer shall then act as President, and such Officer shall act accordingly, until the Disability be removed, or a President shall be elected.

(Compensation)

The President shall, at stated Times, receive for his Services, a Compensation, which shall neither be increased nor diminished during the Period for which he shall have been elected, and he shall not receive within that Period any other Emolument from the United States, or any of them.

(Oath of Office)

Before he enter on the Execution of his office, he shall take the following Oath or Affirmation:—"I do solemnly swear (or affirm) that I will faithfully execute the Office of the President of the United States, and will to the best of my Ability, preserve, protect and defend the Constitution of the United States."

(Powers of the President)

Section 2. The President shall be Commander in Chief of the Army and Navy of the United States, and of the Militia of the several States, when called into the actual Service of the United States; he may require the Opinion, in writing, of the principal Officer in each of the executive Departments, upon any Subject relating to the Duties of their respective Offices, and he shall have Power to grant Reprieves and Pardons for Offenses against the United States, except in Cases of Impeachment.

(Making of Treaties)

He shall have Power, by and with the Advice and Consent of the Senate, to make Treaties, provided two thirds of the Senators present concur; and he shall nominate, and by and with the Advice and Consent of the Senate, shall appoint Ambassadors, other public Ministers and Consuls, Judges of the supreme Court, and all other Officers of the United States, whose Appointments are not herein otherwise provided for, and which shall be established by Law: but Congress may by Law vest the Appointment of such inferior Officers, as they think proper, in the President alone, in the Courts of Law, or in the Heads of Departments.

(Vacancies)

The President shall have Power to fill up all Vacancies that may happen during the Recess of the Senate, by granting Commissions which shall expire at the End of their next Session.

(Additional Duties and Powers)

Section 3. He shall from time to time give to the Congress Information of the State of the Union, and recommend to their Consideration such Measures as he shall judge necessary and expedient; he may, on extraordinary Occasions, convene both Houses, or either of them, and in Case of Disagreement between them, with Respect to the Time of Adjournment, he may adjourn them to such Time as he shall think proper; he shall receive Ambassadors and other public Ministers; he shall take Care that the Laws be faithfully executed, and shall Commission all the Officers of the United States.

(Impeachment)

Section 4. The President, Vice President and all civil Officers of the United States shall be removed from Office on Impeachment for, and Conviction of, Treason, Bribery, or other high Crimes and Misdemeanors.

ARTICLE III ***(Judiciary)***

(Courts, Judges, Compensation)

Section 1. The judicial Power of the United States, shall be vested in one supreme Court, and in such inferior Courts as the Congress may from time to time ordain and establish. The Judges, both of the supreme and inferior Courts, shall hold their Offices during good Behavior, and shall, at stated Times, receive for their Services, a Compensation which shall not be diminished during their Continuance in Office.

(Jurisdiction)

Section 2. The judicial Power shall extend to all Cases, in Law and Equity, arising under this Constitution, the Laws of the United States, and Treaties made, or which shall be made, under their Authority—to all Cases affecting Ambassadors, other public Ministers and Consuls;—to all Cases of admiralty and maritime Jurisdiction;—to Controversies to which the United States shall be a Party;—to Controversies between two or more States;—*between a State and Citizens of another State;*—between Citizens of different States;—between Citizens of the same State claiming Lands under Grants of different States, and between a State, or the Citizens thereof, and foreign States, Citizens or Subjects.

In all Cases affecting Ambassadors, other public Ministers and Consuls, and those in which a State shall be Party, the Supreme Court shall have original Jurisdiction. In all the other Cases before mentioned, the supreme Court shall have appellate Jurisdiction, both as to Law and Fact, with such Exceptions, and under such Regulations as the Congress shall make.

(Trial by Jury)

The Trial of all Crimes, except in Cases of Impeachment, shall be by Jury; and such Trial shall be held in the State where said Crimes shall have been committed; but when not committed within any State, the Trial shall be at such Place or Places as the Congress may by Law have directed.

(Treason)

Section 3. Treason against the United States, shall consist only in levying War against them, or in adhering to their Enemies, giving them Aid and Comfort. No Person shall be convicted of Treason unless on the Testimony of two Witnesses to the same overt Act, or on Confession in open Court.

The Congress shall have Power to declare the Punishment of Treason, but no Attainder of Treason shall work Corruption of Blood, or Forfeiture except during the Life of the Person attained.

ARTICLE IV ***(Federal System)***

Section 1. Full Faith and Credit shall be given in each State to the public Acts, Records, and judicial Proceedings of every other State. And the Congress may by general Laws prescribe the Manner in which such Acts, Records, and Proceedings shall be proved, and the Effect thereof.

(Privileges and Immunities of Citizens)

Section 2. The Citizens of each State shall be entitled to all Privileges and Immunities of Citizens in the several States.

A Person charged in any State with Treason, Felony, or other Crime, who shall flee from Justice, and be found in another State, shall on Demand of the executive Authority of the State from which he fled, be delivered up, to be removed to the State having Jurisdiction of the crime.

No Person held to Service or Labor in one State, under the Laws thereof, escaping into another, shall, in Consequence of any Law or Regulation therein, be discharged from such Service or Labor, but shall be delivered up on Claim of the Party to whom such Service or Labor may be due.

(Admission and Formation of New States; Governing of Territories)

Section 3. New States may be admitted by the Congress into this Union; but no new State shall be formed or erected within the Jurisdiction of any other State; nor any State be formed by the Junction of two or more States, or Parts of States, without the Consent of the Legislatures of the States concerned as well as of the Congress.

The Congress shall have Power to dispose of and make all needful Rules and Regulations respecting the Territory or other Property belonging to the United States; and nothing in this Constitution shall be so construed as to Prejudice any Claims of the United States, or of any particular State.

(Federal Protection of the States)

Section 4. The United States shall guarantee to every State in this Union a Republican Form of Government, and shall protect each of them against Invasion; and on Application of the Legislature, or of the Executive (when the Legislature cannot be convened), against domestic Violence.

ARTICLE V ***(Amendments)***

The Congress, whenever two thirds of both Houses shall deem it necessary, shall propose Amendments to this Constitution, or, on the Application of the Legislatures of two thirds of the several States, shall call a Convention for proposing Amendments, which, in either Case, shall be valid to all Intents and Purposes, as Part of this Constitution, when ratified by the legislatures of three fourths of the several States, or by Conventions in three fourths thereof, as the one or the other Mode of Ratification may be proposed by the Congress; Provided *that no Amendments which may be made prior to the Year One thousand eight hundred and eight shall in any Manner affect the first and fourth Clauses in the Ninth Section of the first Article; and* that no State, without its Consent, shall be deprived of its equal Suffrage in the Senate.

ARTICLE VI ***(Constitution as Supreme Law)***

All Debts contracted and Engagements entered into, before the Adoption of this Constitution, shall be as valid against the United States under this Constitution, as under the Confederation.

This Constitution, and the Laws of the United States which shall be made in Pursuance thereof; and all Treaties made, or which shall be made, under the Authority of the United States, shall be the supreme Law of the Land, and the Judges in every State shall be bound thereby, any Thing in the Constitution or Laws of any State to the Contrary notwithstanding.

The Senators and Representatives before mentioned, and the Members of the several State Legislatures, and all executive and judicial Officers, both of the United States and of the several States, shall be bound by Oath or Affirmation, to support this Constitution; but no religious Test shall ever be required as a Qualification to any Office or public Trust under the United States.

ARTICLE VII ***(Ratification)***

The Ratification of the Conventions of nine States shall be sufficient for the Establishment of the Constitution between the States so ratifying the same.

Done in Convention by the Unanimous Consent of the States present, the Seventeenth Day of September in the Year of our Lord one thousand seven hundred and Eighty seven and of the Independence of the United States of America the Twelfth. In witness whereof We have hereunto subscribed our Names.

Geo. Washington, *President and deputy from Virginia; Attest* William Jackson, *Secretary; Delaware:* Geo. Read, Gunning Bedford, Jr., John Dickinson, Richard Bassett, Jaco. Broom; *Maryland:* James McHenry, Daniel of St. Thomas Jenifer, Danl. Carroll; *Virginia:* John Blair, James Madison, Jr.; *North Carolina:* Wm. Blount, Richd. Dobbs Spaight, Hu Williamson; *South Carolina:* J. Rutledge, Charles Cotesworth Pinckney, Charles Pinckney, Pierce Butler; *Georgia:* William Few, Abr. Baldwin; *New Hampshire:* John Langdon, Nicholas Gilman; *Massachusetts:* Nathaniel Gorham, Rufus King; *Connecticut:* Wm. Saml. Johnson, Roger Sherman; *New York:* Alexander Hamilton; *New Jersey:* Wil. Livingston, David Brearley, Wm. Paterson, Jona. Dayton; *Pennsylvania:* B. Franklin, Thomas Mifflin, Robt. Morris, Geo. Clymer, Thos. FitzSimons, Jared Ingersoll, James Wilson, Gouv. Morris.

AMENDMENTS TO THE CONSTITUTION

(The first ten amendments are known as the Bill of Rights.)

AMENDMENT I [1791] ***(Freedoms)***

(Speech, Press, Assembly, and Petition)

Congress shall make no law respecting an establishment of religion, or prohibiting the free exercise thereof; or abridging the freedom of speech, or of the press; or the right of the people peaceably to assemble, and to petition the Government for a redress of grievances.

AMENDMENT II [1791] ***(Right to Bear Arms)***

A well regulated Militia, being necessary to the security of a free State, the right of the people to keep and bear Arms, shall not be infringed.

AMENDMENT III [1791] ***(Quartering of Soldiers)***

No Soldier shall, in time of peace be quartered in any house, without the consent of the Owner, nor in time of war, but in a manner to be prescribed by law.

AMENDMENT IV [1791] ***(Freedom of Persons)***

(Warrants, Searches, and Seizure)

The right of the people to be secure in their persons, houses, papers, and effects, against unreasonable searches and seizures, shall not be violated, and no Warrants shall issue, but upon probable cause, supported by Oath or Affirmation, and particularly describing the place to be searched, and the persons or things to be seized.

AMENDMENT V [1791] ***(Capital Crimes)***

(Protection of the Accused; Compensation)

No person shall be held to answer for a capital, or otherwise infamous crime, unless on a presentment or indictment of a Grand Jury, except in cases arising in the land or naval forces, or in the Militia, when in actual service in time of War or public danger; nor shall any person be subject for the same offense to be twice put in jeopardy of life or limb; nor shall be compelled in any criminal case to be a witness against himself, nor be deprived of life, liberty, or property, without due process of law; nor shall private property be taken for public use, without just compensation.

AMENDMENT VI [1791] ***(Trial by Jury)***

(Accusation, Witnesses, Counsel)

In all criminal prosecutions, the accused shall enjoy the right to a speedy and public trial, by an impartial jury of the State and district wherein the crime shall have been committed, which district shall have been previously ascertained by law, and to be informed of the nature and cause of the accusation; to be confronted with the witnesses against him; to have compulsory process for obtaining Witnesses in his favor, and to have the assistance of counsel for his defense.

AMENDMENT VII [1791] ***(Civil Law)***

In Suits at common law, where the value in controversy shall exceed twenty dollars, the right of trial by jury shall be preserved, and no fact tried by a jury, shall be otherwise re-examined in any court of the United States, than according to the rules of the common law.

AMENDMENT VIII [1791] ***(Bails, Fines, and Punishments)***

Excessive bail shall not be required, nor excessive fines imposed, nor cruel and unusual punishments inflicted.

AMENDMENT IX [1791] ***(Rights Retained by the People)***

The enumeration in the Constitution, of certain rights, shall not be construed to deny or disparage others retained by the people.

AMENDMENT X [1791] ***(Rights Reserved to the States)***

The powers not delegated to the United States by the Constitution, nor prohibited by it to the States, are reserved to the States respectively, or to the people.

AMENDMENT XI [1798] ***(Jurisdictional Limits)***

The Judicial power of the United States shall not be construed to extend to any suit in law or equity, commenced or prosecuted against one of the United States by Citizens of another State, or by Citizens or Subjects of any Foreign State.

AMENDMENT XII [1804] ***(Electoral College)***

The Electors shall meet in their respective States, and vote by ballot for President and Vice-President, one of whom, at least, shall not be an inhabitant of the same State with themselves; they shall name in their ballots the person voted for as President, and in distinct ballots the person voted for as Vice-President, and they shall make distinct lists of all persons voted for as President, and of all persons voted for as Vice-President, and of the number of votes for each, which lists they shall sign and certify, and transmit sealed to the seat of the government of the United States, directed to the President of the Senate;—The President of the Senate shall, in the presence of the Senate and House of Representatives, open all the certificates and the votes shall then be counted;—The person having the greatest number of votes for President, shall be the President, if such number be a majority of the whole number of Electors appointed; and if no person have such majority, then from the persons having the highest numbers not exceeding three on the list of those voted for as President, the House of Representatives shall choose immediately, by ballot, the President. But in choosing the President, the votes shall be taken by states, the representation from each state having one vote; a quorum for this purpose shall consist of a member or members from two-thirds of the states, and a majority of all the states shall be necessary to a choice. And if the House of Representatives shall not choose a President whenever the right of choice shall devolve upon them, before *the fourth day of March* next following, then the Vice-President shall act as President, as in the case of the death or other constitutional disability of the President.—The person having the greatest number of votes as Vice-President, shall be the Vice-President, if such number be a majority of the whole number of electors appointed, and if no person have a majority, then from the two highest numbers on the list, the Senate shall choose the Vice-President; a quorum for the purpose shall consist of two-thirds of the whole number of Senators, and a majority of the whole number shall be necessary to a choice. But no person constitutionally ineligible to the office of President shall be eligible to that of Vice-President of the United States.

AMENDMENT XIII [1865] ***(Abolition of Slavery)***

Section 1. Neither slavery nor involuntary servitude, except as a punishment for crime whereof the party shall have been duly convicted, shall exist within the United States, or any place subject to their jurisdiction.

Section 2. Congress shall have power to enforce this article by appropriate legislation.

AMENDMENT XIV [1868] ***(Citizenship)***

(Due Process of Law)

Section 1. All persons born or naturalized in the United States, and subject to the jurisdiction thereof, are citizens of the United States and of the State wherein they reside. No State shall make or enforce any law which shall abridge the privileges or immunities of citizens of the United States; nor shall any State deprive any person of life, liberty, or property, without due process of law; nor deny to any person within its jurisdiction the equal protection of the laws.

(Apportionment; Right to Vote)

Section 2. Representatives shall be apportioned among the several States according to their respective numbers, counting the whole number of persons in each State, excluding Indians not taxed. But when the right to vote at any election for the choice of electors for President and Vice President of the United States, Representatives in Congress, the Executive and Judicial officers of a State, or the members of the Legislature thereof, is denied to any of the male inhabitants of such State, being twenty-one years of age, and citizens of the United States, or in any way abridged, except for participation in rebellion, or other crime, the basis of representation therein shall be reduced in the proportion which the number of such male citizens shall bear to the whole number of male citizens twenty-one years of age in such State.

(Disqualification for Office)

Section 3. No person shall be a Senator or Representative in Congress, or elector of President and Vice President, or hold any office, civil or military, under the United States, or under any State, who, having previously taken an oath, as a member of Congress, or as an officer of the United States, or as a member of any State legislature, or as an executive or judicial officer of any State, to support the Constitution of the United States, shall have engaged in insurrection or rebellion against the same, or given aid or comfort to the enemies thereof. But Congress may by a vote of two-thirds of each House, remove such disability.

(Public Debt)

Section 4. The validity of the public debt of the United States, authorized by law, including debts incurred for payment of pensions and bounties for services in suppressing insurrection or rebellion, shall not be questioned. But neither the United States nor any State shall assume or pay any debt or obligation incurred in aid of insurrection or rebellion against the United States, or any claim for the loss of emancipation of any slave; but all such debts, obligations and claims shall be held illegal and void.

Section 5. The Congress shall have power to enforce, by appropriate legislation, the provisions of this article.

AMENDMENT XV [1870] *(Right to Vote)*

Section 1. The right of citizens of the United States to vote shall not be denied or abridged by the United States or by any State on account of race, color, or previous condition of servitude.

Section 2. The Congress shall have power to enforce this article by appropriate legislation.

AMENDMENT XVI [1913] *(Income Tax)*

The Congress shall have power to lay and collect taxes on incomes, from whatever source derived, without apportionment among the several States, and without regard to any census or enumeration.

AMENDMENT XVII [1913] *(Senators)*

(Election)

The Senate of the United States shall be composed of two Senators from each State, elected by the people thereof, for six years; and each Senator shall have one vote. The electors in each State shall have the qualifications requisite for electors of [voters for] the most numerous branch of the State legislatures.

(Vacancies)

When vacancies happen in the representation of any State in the Senate, the executive authority of such State shall issue writs of election to fill such vacancies: Provided, That the legislature of any State may empower the executive thereof to make temporary appointments until the people fill the vacancies by election as the legislature may direct.

This amendment shall not be so construed as to affect the election or term of any Senator chosen before it becomes valid as part of the Constitution.

AMENDMENT XVIII [1919] *(Prohibition)*

Section 1. *After one year from the ratification of this article the manufacture, sale, or transportation of intoxicating liquors within, the importation thereof into, or the exportation thereof from the United States and all territory subject to the jurisdiction thereof for beverage purposes is hereby prohibited.*

Section 2. *The Congress and the several States shall have concurrent power to enforce this article by appropriate legislation.*

Section 3. *This article shall be inoperative unless it shall have been ratified as an amendment to the Constitution by the legislatures of the several States, as provided by the Constitution, within seven years from the date of the submission thereof to the States by the Congress.*

AMENDMENT XIX [1920] *(Women's Suffrage)*

The right of citizens of the United States to vote shall not be denied or abridged by the United States or by any State on account of sex.

Congress shall have power to enforce this article by appropriate legislation.

AMENDMENT XX [1933] *(Terms of Office)*

Section 1. The terms of the President and Vice President shall end at noon on the 20th day of January, and the terms of Senators and Representatives at noon on the 3d day of January, of the years in which such terms would have ended if this article had not been ratified; and the terms of their successors shall then begin.

Section 2. The Congress shall assemble at least once in every year, and such meeting shall begin at noon on the 3d day of January, unless they shall by law appoint a different day.

(Succession)

Section 3. If, at the time fixed for the beginning of the term of the President, the President elect shall have died, the Vice President elect shall become President. If a President shall not have been chosen before the time fixed for the beginning of his term, or if the President elect shall have failed to qualify, then the Vice President elect shall act as President until a President shall have qualified; and the Congress may by law provide for the case wherein neither a President elect nor a Vice President elect shall have qualified, declaring who shall then act as President, or the manner in which one who is to act shall be selected, and such persons shall act accordingly until a President or Vice President shall have qualified.

Section 4. The Congress may by law provide for the case of the death of any of the persons from whom the House of Representatives may choose a President whenever the right of choice shall have devolved upon them, and for the case of the death of any of the persons from whom the Senate may choose a Vice President whenever the right of choice shall have devolved upon them.

Section 5. Sections 1 and 2 shall take effect on the 15th day of October following the ratification of this article.

Section 6. This article shall be inoperative unless it shall have been ratified as an amendment to the Constitution by the legislatures of three-fourths of the several States within seven years from the date of its submission.

AMENDMENT XXI [1933] *(Prohibition Repealed)*

Section 1. The eighteenth article of amendment to the Constitution of the United States is hereby repealed.

Section 2. The transportation or importation into any State, Territory, or Possession of the United States for delivery or use therein of intoxicating liquors, in violation of the laws thereof, is hereby prohibited.

Section 3. This article shall be inoperative unless it shall have been ratified as an amendment to the Constitution by conventions in the several States, as provided in the Constitution, within seven years from the date of submission thereof to the States by the Congress.

AMENDMENT XXII [1951] *(Term of President)*

Section 1. No person shall be elected to the office of the President more than twice, and no person who has held the office of President, or acted as President, for more than two years of a term to which some other person was elected President shall be elected to the office of the President more than once. But this Article shall not apply to any person holding the office of President when this Article was proposed by the Congress, and shall not prevent any person who may be holding the office of President, or acting as President, during the term within which this Article becomes operative from holding the office of President or acting as President during the remainder of such term.

Section 2. This article shall be inoperative unless it shall have been ratified as an amendment to the Constitution by the legislatures of three-fourths of the several States within seven years from the date of its submission to the States by the Congress.

AMENDMENT XXIII [1961] *(Washington, D.C.)*

(Enfranchisement of Voters in Federal Elections)

Section 1. The District constituting the seat of Government of the United States shall appoint in such manner as the Congress may direct:

A number of electors of President and Vice President equal to the whole number of Senators and Representatives in Congress to which the District would be entitled if it were a State, but in no event more than the least populous State; they shall be in addition to those appointed by the States, but they shall be considered for the purposes of the election of President and Vice President, to be electors appointed by a State; and they shall meet in the District and perform such duties as provided by the twelfth article of amendment.

Section 2. The Congress shall have power to enforce this article by appropriate legislation.

AMENDMENT XXIV [1964] *(Poll Tax)*

Section 1. The right of citizens of the United States to vote in any primary or other election for President or Vice President, for electors for President or Vice President, or for Senator or Representatives in Congress, shall not be denied or abridged by the United States or any State by reason of failure to pay any poll tax or other tax.

Section 2. The Congress shall have power to enforce this article by appropriate legislation.

AMENDMENT XXV [1967] *(Succession)*

Section 1. In case of the removal of the President from office or of his death or resignation, the Vice President shall become President.

Section 2. Whenever there is a vacancy in the office of the Vice President, the President shall nominate a Vice President who shall take office upon confirmation by a majority vote of both Houses of Congress.

Section 3. Whenever the President transmits to the President pro tempore of the Senate and the Speaker of the House of Representatives his written declaration that he is unable to discharge the powers and duties of his office, and until he transmits to them a written declaration to the contrary, such powers and duties shall be discharged by the Vice President as Acting President.

Section 4. Whenever the Vice President and a majority of either the principal officers of the executive departments or of such other body as Congress may by law provide, transmit to the President pro tempore of the Senate and the Speaker of the House of Representatives their written declaration that the President is unable to discharge the powers and duties of his office, the Vice President shall immediately assume the powers and duties of the office as Acting President.

Thereafter, when the President transmits to the President pro tempore of the Senate and the Speaker of the House of Representatives his written declaration that no inability exists, he shall resume the powers and duties of his office unless the Vice President and a majority of either the principal officers of the executive department or of such other body as Congress may by law provide, transmit within four days to the President pro tempore of the Senate and the Speaker of the House of Representatives their written declaration that the President is unable to discharge the powers and duties of his office. Thereupon Congress shall decide the issue, assembling within forty-eight hours for that purpose if not in session. If the Congress, within twenty-one days after receipt of the latter written declaration, or, if Congress is not in session, within twenty-one days after Congress is required to assemble, determines by two-thirds vote of both Houses that the President is unable to discharge the powers and duties of his office, the Vice President shall continue to discharge the same as Acting President; otherwise, the President shall resume the powers and duties of his office.

AMENDMENT XXVI [1971] *(18-Year-Old Vote)*

Section 1. The right of citizens of the United States, who are eighteen years of age or older, to vote shall not be denied or abridged by the United States or by any State on account of age.

Section 2. The Congress shall have power to enforce this article by appropriate legislation.

AMENDMENT XXVII [1992] *(Congressional Pay Raises)*

No law, varying the compensation for the services of the Senators and Representatives, shall take effect, until an election of Representatives shall have intervened.

Answer Keys

The Articles of Confederation (pages 5–6)

1. YES. There were few newspapers, and people were unaware of what was happening or not happening in Congress.
2. NO. The president of Congress merely presided over its sessions. He was not considered the leader of the nation by anyone.
3. NO. The Articles gave Congress the power to make treaties.
4. NO. Congress had no taxing power.
5. NO. They seldom had a quorum to pass anything, and there were few accomplishments except the Land Ordinance (1785) and the Northwest Ordinance (1787).
6. NO. Congress could only ask for money from states; it had no power to demand that states pay their share of the expenses.
7. NO. There were no Confederation judges.
8. YES. In the peace treaty, the British promised to withdraw with all convenient speed. They did not do it, and the United States was too weak to make them leave.
9. NO. Shay's Rebellion was composed of poor, not rich, people.
10. YES. Many of those chosen never went for that reason.

Calling the Consitutional Convention (page 9)

1–3. Various reasons might be given: family pressures, financial responsibilities, not being given the power to make any decisions, lack of quorums, listening to complaints.

4. New Jersey was angry over the New York tax (tariff) on eggs imported from other states.
5. Jay was very unpopular in the West for making a treaty with Spain that would keep them from using the Mississippi River.
6. The big states thought that since they had more people and more wealth they should have more voice than the small states.
7. The Mount Vernon Conference met to discuss trade on the Potomac River.
8. The Annapolis Convention failed because so few states were represented.
9. Hamilton wanted a strong national government.
10. They were good at compromise, and that made it possible to settle differences.

Drafting and Ratifying the Constitution (page 12)

1. 55
2. James Madison
3. Legislative, executive, and judicial
4. Republican government derives its authority from the people and must answer to them.
5. Each state having an equal number
6. Representation based on population
7. The House of Representatives was to be chosen on the basis of population; each state was to have an equal number of senators.
8. Senators serve six years; members of the House serve two-year terms.
9. Electors are equal to the number of representatives and senators.
10. Anti-Federalists opposed the Constitution.

Understanding the Constitution (page 15)

1. No. Bills require approval by a majority in both houses.
2. The president can veto a bill; he sends it to the house where it originated.
3. Two-thirds vote of both houses
4. To allow each branch of government to operate free from intrusion by the others
5. By impeachment by the house and being found guilty in a Senate trial
6. No. Only the federal government is allowed to make treaties.
7. "Elastic clause"
8. Yes, but only with the approval of your state.
9. Amendments require a two-thirds vote of both houses.
10. Three-fourths of the states must approve before it is ratified.

Pre-Quiz on Article I, Sections 1–6 (page 19)

1. Article I, Section 2, Paragraph 4
2. Article I, Section 2, Paragraph 2
3. Article I, Section 4, Paragraph 2
4. Article I, Section 6, Paragraph 2
5. Article I, Section 6, Paragraph 1
6. Article I, Section 3, Paragraph 7
7. Article I, Section 3, Paragraph 6
8. Article I, Section 3, Paragraph 6

Answer Keys

Pre-Quiz on Article I, Sections 7–10 (page 24)

1. NO Article I, Section 9, Paragraph 3
2. YES Article I, Section 8, Paragraph 5
3. YES Article I, Section 7, Paragraph 2
4. YES Article I, Section 8, Paragraph 13
5. NO Article I, Section 9, Paragraph 5
6. NO Article I, Section 10, Paragraph 3
7. YES Article I, Section 8, Paragraph 2
8. NO Article I, Section 7, Paragraph 1

Pre-Quiz on Article II, Section 1 (page 27)

1. NO Paragraph 1
2. YES Paragraph 5
3. NO Paragraph 7
4. NO Paragraph 2
5. YES Paragraph 5
6. YES Paragraph 2
7. NO Paragraph 4
8. YES Paragraph 7

Pre-Quiz on Article II, Sections 2–4 (page 31)

1. YES Section 2, Paragraph 1
2. NO Section 2, Paragraph 2
3. YES Section 3, Paragraph 1
4. YES Section 4, Paragraph 1
5. NO Section 2, Paragraph 2
6. YES Section 2, Paragraph 1
7. YES Section 3, Paragraph 1
8. YES Section 4, Paragraph 1

Pre-Quiz on Article III (page 34)

1. NO Section 2, Paragraph 1 or 2
2. NO Section 1, Paragraph 1
3. NO Section 2, Paragraph 3
4. YES Section 2, Paragraph 1
5. NO Section 1, Paragraph 1
6. YES Section 2, Paragraph 1 or Section 3, Paragraph 1
7. YES Section 3, Paragraph 1
8. NO Section 3, Paragraph 2

Pre-Quiz on Articles IV–VII (page 37)

1. NO Article IV, Section 2, Paragraph 1
2. NO Article VI, Section 1, Paragraph 2
3. YES Article IV, Section 3, Paragraph 1
4. NO Article V, Section 1, Paragraph 1
5. YES Article IV, Section 2, Paragraph 2
6. NO Article VI, Section 1, Paragraph 3
7. NO Article VI, Section 1, Paragraph 1
8. NO Article IV, Section 1, Paragraph 1

Pre-Quiz on Amendments 1–5 (page 40)

1. Amendment 1
2. Amendment 5
3. Amendment 5
4. Amendment 2
5. Amendment 1
6. Amendment 3
7. Amendment 4
8. Amendment 1

Pre-Quiz on Amendments 6–12 (page 43)

1. Amendment 7
2. Amendment 12
3. Amendment 8
4. Amendment 9
5. Amendment 6
6. Amendment 12
7. Amendment 6
8. Amendment 8

Pre-Quiz on Amendments 13–15 (page 46)

1. Amendment 13
2. Amendment 15
3. Amendment 14
4. Amendment 13
5. Amendment 14
6. Amendment 14
7. Amendment 15
8. Amendment 14

Pre-Quiz on Amendments 16–21 (page 49)

1. Amendment 19
2. Amendment 17
3. Amendment 16
4. Amendment 18
5. Amendment 20
6. Amendment 21
7. Amendment 17
8. Amendment 20

Pre-Quiz on Amendments 22-27 (page 52)

1. Amendment 26
2. Amendment 24
3. Amendment 25
4. Amendment 23
5. Amendment 27
6. Amendment 22
7. Amendment 25
8. Amendment 22

Answer Keys

Missing Words From the Constitution (pages 53–54)

1. Union
2. Defense
3. Congress
4. Seven
5. Vice President
6. Senate
7. House of Representatives
8. Two
9. Executive
10. Commander-in-chief
11. State of the Union
12. Supreme Court
13. Republican
14. Two-thirds
15. Supreme

Memory Check (page 54)

1. 90 (25 for representative, 30 for senator, 35 for president)
2. 67 (two-thirds)
3. 218 (half)

Missing Words From the Amendments (page 55)

1. Religion
2. Searches
3. Speedy
4. Bail
5. Slavery
6. January
7. Twice
8. Eighteen

Answers to the Constitution Test

Section 1 (page 56)

1. I
2. D
3. F
4. N
5. H
6. J
7. B
8. P
9. E
10. G
11. O
12. C
13. M
14. L
15. A

Section 2 (page 57)

1. F
2. F
3. T
4. T
5. F
6. T
7. F
8. T
9. T
10. F
11. T
12. F
13. T
14. F
15. T
16. T
17. F
18. T
19. F
20. F

Section 3 (pages 58–59)

1. B
2. C
3. A
4. B
5. C
6. C
7. A
8. B
9. C
10. B
11. C
12. A
13. B
14. B
15. A
16. A
17. C
18. B
19. A
20. B

Section 4 (page 59)

1. M
2. S
3. S
4. S
5. M

Section 5 (page 60)

1. E
2. C
3. D
4. A
5. B

Section 6 (page 60)

1. A
2. A
3. A
4. A
5. A